CORNBREAD MEMORIES:
Home of Cotton, Catfish, and Hot Tamales!

Stories from the heart about growing up in the Mississippi Delta by

Ron Kattawar

Acknowledgements

First, I want to thank the many Greenville friends (and Facebook's new friends), along with Charles Betterton, that encouraged me to write this book. It's their belief in me that kept me at task.

Next, my best friend and wife, Carol Cauley Kattawar, who patiently gave her approving nod, knowing a writer becomes absent for a time.

A close and treasured friend, Danny Thomas, spent endless hours correcting my mistakes. It's Danny's critical eye that we can all thank for amazing edits and clean copy.

A very special thank you to my beautiful daughter, Kim Kattawar Mahfouz, a published writer and patient friend that applied her expertise to finalize the project. I would have been lost without her.

And lastly, a very special friend, Joyce Dixon, who kept me focused on writing and believed in me when my own belief waned.

They are all very special people that have my back. I am truly fortunate and grateful.

Dedication

This book is dedicated to Mike and Dollie Kattawar. No one person could have had better parents.

Table of Contents

Introduction

In September 2013, I was invited to join a Facebook page titled, "Greenville, Ms. - The Way We Remember It." After reading a few memories of fellow Greenvillian's, I decided to write a few of my own.

What a fertile ground to draw on for wonderful childhood memories. Greenville, Mississippi sits midway of Jackson, Mississippi to the south and Memphis, Tennessee to the north. On Lake Ferguson, a tributary of the Mississippi River, Greenville is known for its towboat industry and agriculture including cotton, soybeans and rice.

Per capita, Greenville has more successful literary writers than any other city in America. Well known musicians hail from the area and many claim the Blues originated in Greenville. Artists paint and photograph a culture and scenery that is like no other. We lay claim on the most fertile soil in the world. There's no better for growing great crops. She is a land of colorful, wonderful, indelible people that believe in community.

In 1927, Greenville was flooded and part of the original city remains underwater. To protect and prevent future floods, a large levee was constructed. The levee became a playground for Greenville's youth, including me. Greenville was a small town with a population around fifty thousand. The community, schools and churches were a blend of hard working, friendly people that took the old saying very seriously, "it takes a village to raise a child." Maybe we didn't know everyone, but the community was the perfect size that we knew most everyone.

My youth, the nineteen sixties, was a perfect blend of time, people and places. That created a kid's Utopia of barefoot fishing, lifelong friendships and a host of educators, Firemen, Policemen and community activist that protected us from harm and opened the world to my generation. It was a magical time that I attempt to recapture in the following memories.

The response to the first few memories I posted on Facebook were amazing with many requesting I bring all of my memories together into a book. My intent is to stir memories of every childhood, no matter what the city, one may have grown up. The message is to return to carefree days when life was simple and lived to the fullest.

Within these pages I've shared some cherished family recipes that are an important part of growing up in the Mississippi Delta.

Farmers used to put a slice of cornbread in their pocket as they headed out to the fields to stave off hunger.

I've filled your pockets in the following pages with memories that are intended to stave off hunger for an era now since past. "Cornbread Memories."

Be still and listen. The past is whispering who we are - Ron Kattawar.

CORNBREAD

1 c. self-rising flour
1 c. self-rising cornmeal
¼ c. oil
1 egg
1½ c. buttermilk

Preheat oven to 400*.
Heat oil in pan: sprinkle with a dusting of flour.
Mix all ingredients and pour into pan.
Cook at 400* for 25 minutes or until golden brown.
Using less batter will yield a crunchier cornbread, less thick.

Note: you must have a hot oven and you can't skip the step that heats the oil in the pan. Mom always used Jim Dandy self-rising cornmeal and Gold Medal self-rising flour... not just in her cornbread, but in all of her cooking. I'd walk down a rocky road, barefoot, for a slice of her cornbread!

How to Tune In

I was in the third grade when Dad bought our first TV. I remember it was a high gloss, wooden console with a white glow light around the picture. We were the first in our neighborhood to have a TV and my Dad, being the generous person that he was, invited some of the neighbors over to watch.

That invitation grew and before we knew it, our living room was full of people; some I'm not so sure were neighbors. With six kids, we were already well populated, but when the neighbors came over every evening, our living room was shoulder to shoulder, sitting Indian style, on the crowded floor.

A few weeks into the new TV adventure, Dad being an ardent fan of gizmos and gadgets, proudly announced he had bought the newest thing that would convert our black and white TV to color. It was a thin colored film, much like an x-ray slide that fit over the black and white screen.

It was a deep, lush blue color at the top, grass green color at the bottom and yellow in the middle, which of course turned all the people into an odd looking yellow. The rainbow film lasted about a week before it was retired into the, "almost successful" gizmos/gadget drawer. We went back to black and white and the TV people no longer looked weird with blue hair and yellow or green bodies.

There were not many choices. I think three networks that played mostly variety shows with the likes of Imogene Coca, Phil Silvers and Red Skelton. The TV people inside that wonderful box knew when it was bedtime because an American flag would wave in a breeze and the National Anthem played...followed by a picture of an American Indian head and a high pitched sound that reminded the American audience of Ben Franklin's, "early to bed."

The next gizmo Dad bought was a TV antenna. If you stood at the bottom of the pole and turned it just so...you could pick up another station. There was a lot of shouting from the living room window to outdoors. The grate at the top of the TV antennae looked like four long silver fingers pointing in all four directions.

One of my older brothers pondered if the antenna could pick up air waves. That would mean we were surrounded by mysterious air waves everywhere. He asked how the air waves would affect our bodies. That was the same brother that was always three feet behind the mosquito spray truck, in a full and open run, breathing deep.

He's also the same brother that caught our home on fire with his Christmas chemistry set. No one paid much attention to his air wave theory, except me. I wondered then and wonder now if the air waves do something bad to us.

We had a neighborhood kid that could pick up a radio station through her teeth fillings. If you turned her just so, she was better than a transistor radio. To change channels, you just turned her, kind of like turning the TV antenna. She was pretty popular for a while.

Dad's next gizmo was the rabbit ears. You no longer had to twist and turn the antenna pole. I'm not sure where the aluminum foil thing came in, but I remember the rabbit ears were later covered in it. I guess like that neighbor girl with the teeth fillings that picked up air waves.... those same air waves that are all around us that send pictures and sound through the air...and probably through our bodies if you stood too close. That's the kind of Buck Rogers and Dick Tracy futuristic stuff you always hear about.

As the world moved through all of the technology changes, Dad was there at the leading edge buying one of the first color TVs. Our home had become the movie theater for our family and neighbors until one of our neighbors bought their own TV.

And then it happened! Of all of the innovations and progress towards better TV, Dad brought home the best invention, ever... Jiffy Pop, popcorn!

Be careful what direction you turn your antenna.

Miss Mabel's Religion Court

She used to sit on her front porch and hold court over the entire neighborhood. She was judge, jury and hangman. For the sake of the story, we will call her Mabel...or more to her liking, Miss Mabel.

The reason we can't use her real name is because she knows lawyers and has been known to sic a few of them on friends and relatives and even strangers, depending on their religion.

A good Southern lawyer can smell blood in yesterday's bowl of grits. Some say they can spot a flat, silver dollar two miles down the road with the sun in their eyes. The last thing we want is Miss Mabel lawyering-up by bringing on some dude without socks, in a white suit that speaks in Confederacy, dripping in the question, "How much money does his family have?"

I don't think Miss Mabel meant to be ugly to folks, but you never know. She may have been just plain mean to the bone. You decide.

Kirby lived a few blocks away and the first time he came over to our neighborhood he found himself before Judge Mabel.

"What's your name, boy?"

"Kirby, ma'am."

And just what does your father do?"

I ain't got no father."

"I see."

Miss Mabel worked her way to the defining question that always determined if you were "worthy" or not.

"And to which church does your family attend?"

"Baptist, I think, ma'am."

"That's good. You go along and play with the kids now."

Kirby passed Miss Mabel's test. He was a good old Southern Baptist.

If you were Methodist, according to Miss Mabel, you were being drawn in the wrong direction and need to reconsider coming back to the Baptist fold. If you were Catholic, there's no hope for you.

You're going to Hell and no way out of it. Fact is, anyone that wasn't Baptist was condemned to Hell, forevermore. That's just the way it is in Miss Mabel's court.

People would walk by her home and I heard words I didn't understand. "Charlatan" was way beyond my pay grade at ten years old. "Hustler" I knew. You can't be around a good marble game and not know what a hustler is.

Other things she said just simply escaped me or any logic like, "evil as sin". When you're evil you have to be sinning, so I guess I just didn't get the connection. Miss Mabel was a colorful character that opened her mouth and trash just fell out.

I had an uncle that was so deep rooted in Southern Baptist he asked me one day. "Ain't you Catholic?"

"Yes sir, I am."

"Ain't you the ones that put Christ up on the cross?"
"No sir. I think that was the Romans."

Of course he was confused by my answer and told me, kids weren't supposed to smart off to adults. As you can tell, there's no reasoning with some people...which brings us back to Miss Mabel.

She had two sons about our age and the youngest had a cackle-laugh. We used to tackle him and tickle him until he cackled. Weirdest thing, the way he laughed, somewhere between a horse whinny and a cat meowing.

It was worth what we knew was coming, and that was Miss Mabel standing at the porch edge, hands on hips, demanding we let her son up. When she was worked up her voice sounded more like a demon from a scary movie. She could send Boris Karloff to bed without supper.

One time we tickled that kid too much. He did cackle, but when we let him up the front of his pants were wet. I pretended like I didn't see it. He ran in his house and we didn't see him for a few days. Miss Mabel would have stewed us for supper if she had known what we did to her son.

She hated anyone that wasn't Baptist. She would fan herself with her paper church fan, hum what I think may have been church songs and rock as she surveyed the neighborhood, stopping just long enough to make her judgment of anyone that dared walk in front of her porch.

We all know folks like Miss Mabel. As I got older I realized she wasn't alone in her encapsulated world. My Uncle, Bless him, never asked me about the Catholic Church, again...but I did something he would never do...I visited other churches. No one has a monopoly.

As a small child one of my favorite things to do was take a road trip with my Grandmother. I don't think she ever drove over thirty and a trip from Greenville to Natchez was an eternity. Back then, the only thing air conditioned was the Paramount and maybe Kroger's. I can tell you her car sure wasn't air conditioned. She wasn't much for letting me hang my head out the window either.

Her sister, Aunt Annie, was a devout Catholic. Her backyard bumped the backyard of the Catholic Church. She had cut a rutted path from her home to the church, going every day, sometimes more than once, always with a black lace head covering.

Now there are only a few places on earth that I've encountered that have affected me in a way that feels spiritual. One such place is a small island off the coast of Bermuda. St. Charles is a small island about three football fields long and maybe two football fields wide that has a 1600's British fort that still remains. Above the fort is a peak, the tallest part of the island. It's there, where the salt air, the strong breeze, and waves crashing to the rocks below that you feel it.

All things that matter, anything significant folds into one. The wide open ocean to one side and a breath-taking blue lagoon on the other. It's such a place that Baptist, Catholic, or Methodist doesn't matter. God speaks to you there.

The church in Natchez is St. Mary's Basilica. When you walk in the venerable church you feel God's arms embrace you.

And the last of my three special places is St. Joseph's Catholic Church, in Greenville. God is there waiting for you and when you arrive, you both know it. It's the place Carol and I took our vows. It's also a place that I enjoy, alone.

No Mass, no lecture, no priest. One on one. It's a Holy place that Miss Mabel should have enjoyed. It's a Holy place that Miss Mabel and my Uncle could have enjoyed. Blinders are hurtful. It doesn't matter what's written on the door. Sometimes there isn't a door. What matters is who is talking and who is listening.

Miss Mabel's court is adjourned.

Big Brothers and Rocks

Big brothers; sometimes means big trouble. Constant picking, nagging and testing. Big brothers also mean someone you can go to and share inner-most secrets or get advice. Don't expect tears and hugs. That's what big sisters do.

My brother two years older than I, was put on this earth to aggravate and irritate me. At least at times I sure felt like it. He was the A&I master. Maybe I was an easy target because in spite of his never-ending harassing, I followed him around like a little puppy.

He would put on his pair of skates and let out in a hearty stride from Walnut Street to Poplar on the bumpy Alexander Street sidewalk. I was usually on my one skate fifteen feet behind, pumping twice as hard. I often wondered if he hid my other skate out of boyish meanness, or to make sure I couldn't keep up with him.

His friends would come by, bat and glove in hand and invite him to play baseball under a large ancient tree beside Susie Trigg Elementary, on the levee side. Ball had been played there so often, the baselines were ingrain into the dirt. There was literally a permanent baseball diamond worn into the earth. The large tree was one of those, "since time began trees", we were accustomed to seeing in childhood. The limbs were bigger than the trees we see today. Eight of us hooked hands and we couldn't reach around that massive tree.

As my brother and his buddies headed off to the ball

field, I kept a distance and tagged along. I was too little and too young to play but I still went. It's what little brothers do no matter how many rocks are thrown.

The guys would warm up, some would bat while others fielded. Now if you aren't from Greenville, you may have some difficulty understanding. Early 1960s, racial strife and the bad rap our State had for racial tensions were not in our vocabulary or in our hearts. Here's the story, you decide how you want to react to it.

As the guys warmed up, a group of black kids would show up from the close-by neighborhood. Yes, they had their own neighborhood. Greenville was segregated. Schools, churches, towns and neighborhoods were either black or white. There would be a coin toss, deciding first bat...and the game was on.

It was us against them, but not in the sense one may think. I chose to believe it was our neighborhood against another. There was no anger, no name calling, and no fighting. It was simply athlete pitted against athlete. Sometimes my brother's team won, sometimes not. What you could count on was a spirited game, where both teams gave their all.

Now, before you allow your mind to go wandering off and thinking that one team had better equipment, I should stop here and tell you that we were all poor, black and white. Well, except for the one kid that owned the bat. We all thought he was rich because he had a bat. So don't think it was a game of best equipment. The team that brought the most energy and talent to the field, won.

In our home, we were not allowed to use the N bomb. We were taught respect for everyone and my Mom, Bless her, told us all early-on to judge the fruit, not the tree. Of course, I was near-adult before I understood what that meant.

An odd thing happened at one of those ballgames. For a lack of better words, I'll simply call it the "little brothers club." Short, too young to play, kids gathered and watched the older brothers play ball. Little did we realize, in a couple of years, we would be the ones on the ball field, playing our own games. Friendships grew as we taught and learned the basics of baseball.

Watching our older brother's play was better than what any coach could teach. To become a good player you have to have the passion and love of the game...and that's where it all begins. Little brothers, both black and white, absorbed baseball and we learned from each other. As we got older, girls began showing up to watch the big brother's game and that's the time the older brothers started acting weird. Doing stupid things.

My brother was no exception. He climbed up the massive tree trunk and onto one of its arms. Maybe thinking that wasn't enough to impress, he walked out further onto the limb as if he were a circus tightrope acrobat. He stumbled and fell flat on his back, knocking the air out of him. I was the first one there. He wasn't breathing and was purple around his lips. I can't remember ever being so scared. When he opened his eyes, I wanted to hit him.

One of the black boys ran to his home and got a jug of water and a cloth. My brother, more embarrassed than hurt, recognized the injury as an interesting attention getter and played it to the hilt for his concerned female audience. Ten minutes later he was hitting a double bringing in one runner.

I never knew that young boy's name that went for water, but I would like to thank him for what he did for my brother. My mama would say his tree bears good fruit.

As an adult and looking back on those days, I have to say, I didn't see anger and hate. I did see a divided community but never gave it any thought. It was the world as it was and certainly not as the news media wanted to convey. I remember the coming years were troubling to me. My experience of playing baseball, white against black never developed into anything more or anything less than a spirited ball game that ended in a friendly handshake or high five with each of the opposing team members. Due respect earned and acknowledged.

A lot has changed since. Decades later Carol and I had just moved to Cincinnati. Great timing: from four years in beautiful Bermuda to a four foot snow, didn't start our experience of living up North as a good start. The first week of clear weather, we decided to explore the "city." It was there in the main street of Cincinnati, we became trapped in the traffic flow because of a parade. That was the first time I had witnessed a KKK parade, seen a white hood or seen the anger and hatred.

There I am in sure-nuff, Yankee-land and what is before me? I couldn't wait to get out of there. I grew up in the bosom of the South; the heart of Dixie, the Divine Delta and never ever...

So much has been heaped on my great State of Mississippi that simply isn't true. So much hate had to be directed and to direct hate you need a target...and that target became Mississippi. It's unjustifiable. It's a lie that will probably never die.

Sometimes it takes a while for the world to make any sense. Sometimes that never happens. I never understood why my older brother was destined to be my tormentor back then and is one of my best friends today.

Or how a community that gently co-existed without hatred was understood as an oppressor. Or how a self-righteous group that has never been saddled with hatred by the media, allowed hooded KKK marchers walk down their main street...in a parade. To get any sense of it all, I rely on my Mom's sage advice.

"Judge the fruit, not the tree....and stop pestering your little brother."

Stuckey's Pecan Roll

Just hearing it makes me want to drive to the Mississippi Bridge, burst into Stuckey's and grab up three of four of those delectable rolls. Of course, Stuckey's is long gone, and all that remains are the memories...and this guy has to have more than just the memories. I want my pecan roll.

Cracker Barrel sells the divine pecan logs. As my hand went out to collect a few, our name was called and if you've ever eaten at Cracker Barrel on Sunday, you know...when your name is called you dash to the desk...or suffer the consequences of another hour wait. There was such a line to pay, I forgot to get a few pecan logs on the way out. Next trip to Cracker Barrel, **I'm promising myself I'll buy double to make up for my missed opportunity.**

In my early twenties, life had tossed a few coins in my direction which gave me the opportunity to drive over the Mississippi Bridge and eat at the Cow Pen. I've wondered if it's still there. I know my stop on this side of the bridge, Stuckey's, is gone. I couldn't do one without the other. A pecan roll before eating at the Cow Pen, and one for after. Perfect meal, perfect dessert. Besides, driving across that bridge wasn't one of my favorite things.

The Mac truck and VW that I witnessed in my earlier years left a few bad memories of crossing a bridge. The poor VW had nowhere to go and was smashed into the side rails of the bridge. It spooked me for years until I wrestled that fear to the ground and defeated it. Driving over bridges doesn't bother me, now, but I wish I had a pecan log to distract me.

Driving to Beaumont, Texas right after my brother had gotten his driver's license added to the bridge thing, for me. We were in Orange, Texas and going literally straight up the side of a bridge. My brother had to push the gas pedal down harder and harder, just to climb this steep mountain of a bridge. As we crest the bridge a Mac truck, whizzed by us at one hundred miles per hour and scared both of us out of three years growth. My brother, Bless him, laughs when he is stressed. He laughed for miles. Tears rolled. I'm not sure about him but I started worrying about going back home and having to take on that straight up bridge, again. No freaky park ride is scarier than that bridge in Orange, Texas.

Inside Stuckey's, if the pecan logs didn't get you, all the exotic and fairly inexpensive gadgets and gizmos, would. I could spend days in that place looking at all of the unusual stuff you didn't see anywhere else.

Cracker Barrel is like that too, but it's always crowded at Cracker Barrel.

One time at Cracker Barrel I talked myself into buying a jar of "homemade" apple pie stuffing for fried apple pies. I'm a sucker for fried apple pies. The instructions were simple, fast and easy. I forgot my Mom's sage advice. "You can taste the short cuts." Like the instructions said, it was fast and easy and tasted...fast and easy. Nothing like my Mom's. I had to re-learn something I've known for years. If you buy fast and easy, you will taste fast and easy. The real thing never includes short cuts.

Going to Stuckey's was always a treat, even as an adult. You mix sugar and pecans...count me in. I'll always buy what the wallet allows.

What I can tell you is this; a perfect day in Greenville would include a stop at Stuckey's, the Cow Pen, Pasquale's, Gino's, Does,' a few slow drives through Strazi's and Dan's B.B.Q. , my parent's graveside, a run by the old homes on Garden Drive and Poplar, and my parent's last home on Main Street. Then on to the wharf, Shipley's Donuts, Ward's Recreation Park, Jim's Cafe, Palace Barber Shop, and everything else in-between. All places that are a part of me and who I am.

They helped shape and define an entire generation that are grateful people that work hard, mind their own business and enjoy life as it comes. We learned respect for our fellow-beings and to help those less fortunate. Ours is a generation of grit-hearty people that meet the challenges and ask, "Is that all you got?"

Greenville's own is a pride unto itself.

Fashion and Pride

When I was in the tenth grade I bought my first car. Hardly a chick-magnet and most certainly not a muscle car. My Ford Falcon was my pride.

I worked at Frostop and earned enough to pay my car payment, car insurance and occasionally had enough for gas. What was important was I had wheels. I could travel. Not far, mind you, maybe a few loops through Dan's Bar B Q and a few loops through Strazi's, then a ride over the levee to see the ducks.

Seeing the ducks was a favorite because it fit well in my tight budget. Free.

What didn't fit in my budget was the passion of my life, at the time; a pair of Italian loafers. Johl and Bergman's, $49.99. Seems like a fair price, but on my limited budget, the distance between me and a pair of Italian loafers grew rather than narrowed.

I had shoes, mind you; and looking back, I could have been grateful, but I wasn't. I wanted a pair of ILS's no matter what. I wanted them bad enough that I let it bug me, daily. Strange how immature minds work. I allowed that pair of shoes to bother me for years to come.

In my senior year I was in Mrs. Wilkerson's Distributive Education class. She was a MSCW beauty, inside and out. She was also one of those people in my life, that I naturally liked. I can't remember ever seeing her without her warm smile. I learned years later the proper word to describe Mrs.

Wilkerson....inclusive. It's a word that would change my life.

She found me a job at Charles Connelly's Shoes inside Stein Mart where I worked for a short, white headed guy named Harry. His wife, ran the cash register. What confused me about them, was that he was Jewish and she was Catholic. I asked him one day how that worked and he said," Simple, Saturday I go to Temple and Sunday she goes to Mass." That was that and never brought up again. Both were really nice people and were always better than nice to me. Carol and I were making plans for our wedding and Harry's wife called me over to give me a small white envelope. She wished Carol and me well in our soon to be wedding.

I was excited and too embarrassed to open the envelope. I knew there must be enough cash to pay for our honeymoon. Later in the day, Harry called me to the stock room and presented me with a shoe box. I had talked so much about Italian loafers, I knew he had gone out of his way and paid a visit to Johl & Bergman's.

I left Stein Mart in such a hurry, I bumped into Jake Stein. He of course had a bundle of jeans over his shoulder. I don't think I ever saw the man without a bundle of something thrown over his shoulder. He and my grandfather were good friends and in their earlier years, had worked together in the "dry goods" business. I apologized for being so clumsy and rushed out to my car. I debated which I should open first, the envelope or the shoe box. I opened the envelope. Shaking hands, I pulled out two single dollar bills. Two dollars! Moving on, I opened the shoe box, hoping to see a dream come true, Italian loafers.

As the lid slid off, I could see it wasn't my dream. Inside the box was a pair of men's house shoes...the left, size 8 1/2 and the right shoe, size 7 1/2. It was no accident that the pair was different sizes. If you ever shopped there, you would understand the concept of seconds and mismatched.

I left the Stein Mart parking lot and drove to my Mom's. I knew she could make some sense of the strange gifts. I was right. For the first time, I heard the word "inclusive" and understood what it meant. In her gentle, loving way she explained that Harry and his wife could have ignored the upcoming wedding and not bothered with a gift. But they didn't. They included me in their lives and wanted me to know I meant something to them.

What was a two dollar gift, became something very special. We didn't spend that two dollars, but put them away with our treasures. The house shoes, I wore, flip-flop for years, until they were well beyond worn out. I had trouble parting with those house shoes. Carol tossed them when I was at work. Some years later, I was maybe in my mid-thirties I walked in my closet to get a pair of shoes. There, on the shoe shelf was not one, not two, but five identical pair of Italian loafers, all brand new. Funny I'd never noticed that before and hadn't worn one pair of them.

It occurred to me that you can't go back and change the past, no matter how many pair of Italian loafers you own. Life is as it is lived and trying to recapture and eliminate that feeling of not belonging because I didn't own a certain pair of shoes became far less important as I got older. That pair of mismatched house shoes that went flip-flop when I walked in them, were far more relative to life and being included in someone's life. The five pair of Italian loafers were donated to Goodwill.

I've never questioned a gift, since. I appreciate whatever it is, from whomever, knowing they Included me in their life and that has far more value than what a gift cost.

When a three year old grandson wraps me a what-not from his grandma's what-not collection and puts it under the Christmas tree, that gift alone is Christmas enough. I've been included in his world and no Italian loafers or fancy gifts can ever match that.

Inclusive.

How to Climb a Tall Man

The YMCA. A small chunk of my youth was spent in that building. I swam, played some heated, do or die ping pong games, learned to shoot pool, made new friends and enjoyed old friends.

The musty, strong chlorine smelling, indoor swimming pool was a place for young and old alike to learn to swim. I was a non-swimmer, scared of the water. Fear can keep you from some of the best times of your life.

Joining the Y program I worked like crazy to earn "Minnow" then worked my way up the fish chain. I slowly overcame my fear of going off the diving board and joined in the double dog dares that followed anyone that raced to go off the diving board next.

Ping pong was another matter. It may seem silly but it was a major, bragging rights game that challenged every fiber of your being. You had to be fast, often very gentle of hand and sometimes when the moment was right a perfect, solid whack would win the game. After a really good game you could be as tired as if you had just run a marathon. No air conditioner, just sweat and pure energy.

I loved my summers at the Y. It was a great place for a kid to learn about responsibility, belonging to a group and self-reliance in individual pursuits like swimming. No doubt the Y shaped a lot of fine young men and women.
As an adult in my mid-thirties I rejoined the Y. They

offered a karate class and I figured, why not? I signed
up Carol, our oldest son and myself. A family thing
we could all do together. It seemed like a good idea.
Carol and our son became ferocious. I tried to be
mister cool.

As in anything new, the moves were awkward and
throwing a punch with a loud "Ke-I" all felt a bit
strange and silly. But as we progressed in class, we
understood the purpose, learned the moves and
became acclimated to our new sport.
One segment of class towards the end was sparring.
We were instructed to utilize our newest move; a
back leg sweep or a back hand punch. The instructor
would have us sit in a circle and as he spun around in
the center he would pick two people to spar.

Now I can be as scrappy as anyone but I never got
the purpose of pairing me with eight foot giants.
Goliath seemed to always show up for class. He was
an awkward guy, hardly nimble or speedy...just tall
enough to bump his head on the ceiling.

The instructor points to me...then Goliath. It almost
became a family joke. My son would ask before class
if I was going to take Goliath down that night. It was
funny...at least until we were facing each other in the
ring and I was looking straight into his navel.

Seems, old Goliath got the back foot sweep down
pretty fast and seconds into our sparring session, the
lights went out. He back swept me with a strong arm
to my shoulder pushing me down onto the extremely
solid hardwood floor with no pads. I recall seeing
stars. No joke...I literally saw stars. That was just

before I lost conscience.

I'm not sure how long I was out but when I woke up Goliath was a few feet away. Now he could have been laughing about what he saw on the Jackie Gleason show, but somehow the timing told me he was tickled that he took me out.

I scrambled to my feet and climbed up that old boy like he was a tree at Delta Pineland. When I was up high enough that my fist could reach his nose, it was my intent to re-arrange it for him. Fist drawn...energy built, heart pumping, adrenaline flowing in full force, I released the wrath of a drunk in a dirt-floor bar.

Inches within his nose, my fist stopped dead cold. It took me a second to realize that my fist was being held in someone's hand. Goliath, had shock on his face. I won't say I scared him, but his face was better than a four hundred page action/adventure novel. I was pulled off that old boy by a very disgusted karate instructor. It was my instructor's hand that prevented the nose punch. He stopped my punch mid-air.

"We're here to learn control! Now give me 100 knuckle pushups!" Funny thing happens to you when you are being punished. Forget the hardwood floor and how tough it was on my knuckles. It's the mind and how it reacts. When you realize you've done something wrong, you have to answer to YOU. I re-played Goliath's nasty back leg sweep. His execution was perfect. My preparedness was lacking. The fall was my fault. Worse, I went after him in anger.

Thinking back, I can say I've never allowed my anger

to reach that boiling point, since. I learned that when something goes wrong, the first person I have to inspect is myself.

Goliath and I never did become good friends. He's probably a pretty good guy. We were made to shake hands at the end of class.

Later that night the instructor told me he had never seen a person climb up a man like that before. I was never sure if that was a compliment or a dig.

I thank my instructor; my brother, for one of life's toughest lessons.

Look to yourself and you will usually find where things went wrong.

Aunt Helen's Secret

Aunt Helen was a small, frail lady that spoke broken English, although she was born in Beaumont, Texas around 1900. She had fiery eyes and spoke fluent dramatics, hitting some words harder than others leaving an unsure trail of exactly what she meant or maybe she slipped off subject.

I met her only once in my early twenties. We spent the day together and what a day that turned out to be! When we were introduced, she wrapped her thin arms around me in a loving, tight squeeze whispering a long Lebanese something or other. I had no idea what she was saying during her lengthy hug.

Now, hugs in a large family are common and at every arrival or departure everyone that is in sight gets a hug; sometimes two hugs, but lengthy hugs with a litany of Lebanese, sort of a chant thing certainly set Aunt Helen a part, right off. I found out later in the day as she talked with a combination of fire and ice, broken English and a mixture of Lebanese dripping in Southern, that when she hugged me she said a prayer of thanks in Lebanese.

She moved in and out of spitfire, depending on standing or sitting. If she were standing and talking it was as if she were trying out for a dramatic role. Seated, she was a bit more subdued using her hands to accent the drama. Oh, she was a trip. An indelible character that you would find deep in a Tennessee Williams play that laughs a lot but you aren't sure what she's laughing about. I loved her uniqueness. Fact is, she wasn't an Aunt or even a family relative.

Not by blood, anyway. Aunt Helen grew up next to one of my Dad's relatives in Beaumont. Dad was taken with their family and over his visits through his younger years, he became a part of their family. It was a relationship that spanned almost nine decades.

As kids, Helen and her seventeen brothers and sisters would insist dad stay for supper, which he laughingly said mealtime was a chaotic feeding of the zoo animals. Helen, burst out in laughter and gave my dad's hand a gentle touch.

"We had so many kids that I'm not sure if my parents even knew your dad was there. He was quiet and bashful, not like us kids always talking over each other in loud voices." You could see the love in her eyes when she talked about dad.

Rose, the relative dad visited, was an amazing cook. During holidays she would cook Lebanese pastries, box them up and send them to us in Greenville. Getting a box from Rose was like a mini-Christmas in and of itself.

Among the various pastries, I discovered Butlawa. Most people know it as Baklava, the Greek name. Butlawa is made a bit different by the old school. Rose wrote the book on old school.

She made phyllo dough from scratch. Dough so thin you could read the newspaper through it. How she did it remains a mystery. Helen told me Rose had clothes lines in her kitchen and hung phyllo dough up to dry. Amazing!

When I told Helen about the box of goodies that Rose sent us for holidays, she was delighted to tell me that Rose used to cook every day and she and her sisters would watch. "We didn't learn how to cook from our mama, she was too busy trying to feed us and didn't have time to teach us how to cook. Rose, she is the one that taught us all how to cook. That lady could make a kitchen sing.

I told Helen that Butlawa was my favorite but Rose passed away so many years ago, we hadn't had Butlawa, since. Rose, took the recipe to her grave.

Helen bounced up from her seat and with both arms lifted in the air she declared, "Then you gotta learn! Let's go to the store and I'll show you what you need!"

Helen couldn't have been five feet tall if you stretched her on the rack. When she got in her Oldsmobile I wondered how she would see over the dash to drive. I'm not sure she ever did. The steering wheel looked like a tractor tire in her tiny hands. I couldn't watch the traffic around us, so I faced her and talked about anything that came to mind...just to stay occupied, hoping we would soon get to Kroger's.

In the store she moved like a bolt of lightning from one area to the next, grabbing up Phyllo Dough from the freezer section and rose water from the exotic aisle and real butter from the dairy aisle. She was on a mission and drove her grocery cart about as well as she drove her eighteen foot long Oldsmobile. I was sixty plus years younger than she and had trouble keeping up with her, so did other shoppers that got in her way.

The drive back to Mom's house on Main Street wasn't as long or tedious. Most folks got out of her way. I was sure glad to see the driveway. She bounced out of that car and was in the house before I could gather up the bags. She rolled up her sleeves and dished out orders like a drill sergeant. I stayed busy following her orders and writing down exactly what she was doing, how much and for how long. Helen's style of cooking is exhausting. She spun in Mom's kitchen like a Tasmanian whirlwind.

Finally, with the final stage, the Butlawa was in the oven and smelled up the entire neighborhood of nectar for the gods...a sweet feast that was about to reacquaint me to a holiday box when I was six years old.

When Helen took those golden brown delicate pastries out of the oven, my mouth watered. The aroma, the sight...so far all the right boxes were ticked. The final test was to taste one...slowly to my mouth, hoping that the taste buds would match the brain's memory. Houston, we got lift off!

What an experience to taste something so incredible for the first time in fifteen years. It was like going home in my memory-mobile. When that butter, phyllo dough and sweet sugar and pecan mixture sat on my tongue...I knew all was right with the world.
It was that day, a day we often refer to as "The Day of Helen." that I knew the stark truth. We had lost a family recipe and were lucky for the day of Helen that it was rediscovered. I made it my priority to never let

that happen again. I spent the next couple of decades shadowing my Mom in her kitchen writing down, videoing and asking stupid questions.

Helen passed a couple of years after her visit. It was the saddest I've ever felt about losing someone that I didn't really know. I stopped wondering how that tiny, cute, soft lady made such a drive from Beaumont to Greenville, and focused on being grateful that she restored a lost, treasured recipe.

The Butlawa recipe is now in every home in our family...and that's a lot of homes. Never, ever to be lost, again.

Pay attention to today, it determines your tomorrow.

Thank you, Helen!

Short Cuts Ruin the Dessert

On the subject of my favorite food that contains all the food groups, let me tell you about my Mom's banana pudding.

To begin with, there's no instant whatever used. Everything is fresh and handmade. I figure if you have to use a box of instant stuff you aren't going to understand - AND that frozen chemical stuff is no topping for the real deal. Egg whites, sugar and a drop of vanilla makes the only suitable topping for a real banana pudding. It needs those huge puffy white globes with a curly on top that melt in your mouth at every bite. It's like biting into clouds of sweetness.

Mom would slip on her apron, over her head, careful not to disturb her hair-do. I guess you could say it was a full body apron. Although she never got anything on her apron, she always wore one.

Thinking about her apron reminds me that you just don't see anyone wear an apron anymore; full body or the waist kind. I pondered on that for a moment and decided you don't need an apron when McDonald's is for supper. Which takes us back to the box of instant verses the real thing. They are sorely connected and forever related.

The filling takes time and patience. Stirring the cooking ingredients requires your full attention...and to get it right, to get it to "jell" just so, requires diligence and practice. The bananas have to be at their height of flavor and only Jack's vanilla wafers will do.

Today, we tap an impatient toe for instant rice in the microwave. We rush from the microwave to make instant tea and eat from paper wrappers and readymade condiments from a small packet. Rush! Rush! And in that process of processing, our taste buds become lazy and tolerant to mediocre. I have an uneasy feeling our lives do the same.

Mom built her banana pudding in slow methodical stages. She often said, "You can taste the hurry ups." That's why she never hurried. No short cuts. According to her, she could taste the short cuts, too. Taste, flavor and whatever it took for that ultimate, she did. Moments of food and family were her passion.

Short cuts, boxes of instant and hurrying cause us to lose quiet moments that used to be shared washing and drying real dishes, hushed talk between people who otherwise wouldn't share the day's news and worst of all, the lost art of table-time. It's traditions we've lost to eating on the fly, in a moving car, at the park or on the way to something that seems all important at the moment. There's not enough time to put a loving pot on the stove top.

Now, I know you are wondering how I can relate a banana pudding to our lives today, but an apron, homemade food and sitting at a table together is what made us, our generation; who we are today. At meal time we heard how our parents survived the Depression or how they survived a lost job or a cog thrown in their lives and how they dealt with it. It was LIFE 101 unfolding at the dinner table...and we had a front row seat.

It is a stark difference of then and now. Today, it is of course, the pace of the race. Instant stuff, drive through and express lanes. There was a time there was no race. No hurry up to do this so we can do that. There was a time when we all sat at the table and relished in a banana pudding made from scratch and filled with patience and love...and that was enough. It filled our tummy and fed our soul and taught us how to deal with the world.

There's an art to it, you know. Making a homemade banana pudding from scratch isn't easy. Neither is life. Sometimes the kitchen gets as messy as our lives. I'm sure that's why some person devised the box of instant...to match the rush, rush, pace of the race. But the essence is lost. LIFE 101 can't be added to liquid and stirred.

That's why sometimes, we being the people that we are, have to get off that merry go round, set the table with real dishes, cook some real food and a real banana pudding and share the conversation table with those that we love.

It's who we are...a people that can taste the short cuts and hunger for the real thing.

BANANA PUDDING

6 large, ripe bananas
1 pkg. Jack's vanilla wafers
3 eggs, separated. (Whites in bowl, yokes in cup)
5 tbsp. self-rising flour
2 c. sugar
½ tsp. vanilla flavoring
3 cups whole milk
Dash of salt

Put flour and sugar in pot and mix. Add salt and milk: stir well. On medium heat, until liquid thickens: add beaten egg yolks by taking a few spoonful of hot mixture and adding to egg yolks in a cup, stir. Do not dump egg yolks in hot mixture, you'll have scrambled eggs. Cook for 8 minutes and turn off heat. Add vanilla flavoring, stir. In a deep baking dish, layer cookies, then bananas and pour enough of mixture to cover the layers. Layer cookies, then bananas, again and pour over remaining mixture.

Note: when adding egg yolks, spoon hot mixture into cup with egg yolks and stir. If you dump 3 egg yolks straight into the hot mixture the eggs will scramble, not blend.

Topping: beat the egg whites thick on low speed. Add 3 tablespoons of sugar while blender is running. Beat, making sure all sugar is absorbed evenly. Add 3 more teaspoons of sugar and repeat. Continue beating mixture until peaks form. Top the pudding with the egg/sugar topping. Cook in oven until the topping browns lightly, about 3-5 minutes.

The Home Fires

Sharon, my cousin, told me that 152 N. Poplar has been demolished recently. Built I think some time in the 1920s, she served families well for almost a century. It's time for her tired bones to rest.

Sitting just off the corners of Poplar and Alexander, she had Williams Grocery to the Alexander side and to her Poplar side, was the mysterious Elks Club.

We moved there as I was finishing the fourth grade at St. Joe. We had a lot going on at that time with moving boxes everywhere and life in an uproar with the move when St. Joe's Principal and Sister Thomas, my teacher, visited our unsettled home. I think their visit was in search of an apology. Seems a Nun's habit doesn't take too well to white chalk. I had stirred up quite a hornet's nest when I returned a thrown chalkboard eraser. I have a pretty good chunking arm and hit my target squarely. I never returned to St. Joe and was registered at Susie P. Trigg.

It wasn't the best way to start off in a new home, but the memory sticks and is used as a measuring stick by myself and siblings of when we moved in. "What year was it that you got hit with an eraser and threw it back at that nun?"

The home had six bedrooms, two baths and a huge kitchen. The living room and dining room flowed from a large front screened-in porch. It was a huge home, with high ceilings and lots of elbow room.

Dad was a superb storyteller and could make up the best stories on the fly. When one of my brothers asked about who lived there before us, Dad told us that a Mrs. Stevens lived there and one stormy night, she died in that house. Made perfectly good sense why doors opened on their own, lights would go off on their own and sometimes we heard her knocking at the front door.

Yep. That house was haunted and we all relished in it, telling Ms. Stevens she didn't scare us. She really didn't until the lights were out and the house got quiet. That's when she bumped through the house opening doors and turning lights on. The best thing to do was pull the pillow up over our faces. If she couldn't see us, she couldn't hurt us.

Back in the day of girls having hope chests, my sister had a cedar hope chest that had some familiarity to a coffin. It was decided that Mrs. Stevens slept in that hope chest. My sister to this day swears she saw the top slowly rise up one night. It was, of course, a stormy night and in a lightning flash the top of Mrs. Steven's coffin opened up. The next day, in calm daylight the cedar chest was relocated. My sister couldn't sleep knowing Mrs. Stevens may come visiting any time it stormed.

One brother's bedroom faced the mysterious Elk Club. In a child's mind, we made up all sorts of crazy and weird things they did in that secret place. They must have been a blood-letting cult or something. Rumor was they took a goat in there that never came back out.

Whatever they did in the Elk's Club didn't matter on steamy, humid afternoons. Neighbors would collect under that bedroom window to listen to my brother practice some "Good Golly" on the piano. One day I remember there must have fifteen or so people sitting on the ground and they had brought a picnic lunch! My brother relished in his random audience and played louder. They were there often and stayed as long as he practiced, which was hours every day.

It was in that house that Dad taught all six of us to play the piano. He was the root, the genesis for our love of music. He would knock out a snappy "Five Foot Two" among his favorite ragtime. Tuesday night we all had to suffer through Lawrence Welk just in the slight hope that Dad would see Joann Castle, a blond woman that would beat the devil out of her ragtime piano. By the time I was in high school I never wanted to see another bubble floating by or hear Lawrence Welk's voice again.

There were a lot of neighbors that have become indelible in the memories associated with that home. The Luncefords, Kathy, Carol and Billie; Nell and Linda Freeman, James and Donnie Dunlap, Barbara Taggart, Duke and Jerry Tobia, Carl and Billie Swilley, Sammy Earl Brown and many, many more all on the ready for a good game of kick the can or chase the mosquito truck.

We had races down the levee riding on flattened out cardboard boxes. Skates, baseball, football, and a rag tag basketball goal. It was days of china berry or dirt clod fights, cowboys and Indians, wild and crazy Halloweens, trick or treating in homemade costumes.

Made up games, rules were applied as we thought them up. We could fight, but it was law that we had to make up before dark. For a group of kids thrown together by happen chance and fate, we had each other's back. Our home, that 152 N. Poplar, was the center of the universe. We always seemed to gather there to begin whatever adventure that day brought us.

Carol and I returned from our honeymoon and stayed in that house for a few weeks, before we bought our first home. That was forty-six years ago, this week.

When I got word the old girl was torn down I sent an email to my siblings which started an avalanche of group emails, all recounting their 152 N. Poplar memories. It was good walking down memory lane with them, reliving special events and times in our lives, anchored to that address. She was more than a building, more than an address, more than a place to hang your hat.

She was a source of life, love and memories.

She was home.

MISSISSIPPI MUD CAKE

1 c. margarine
½ c. cocoa
2 c. sugar
4 eggs, slightly beaten
1½ c. chopped pecans
½ c. flour
1 tsp. Vanilla
1/8 tsp. salt
1/4 bag of small marshmallows

Melt margarine and cocoa together. Remove from heat. Stir in sugar and mix well. Add beaten eggs, flour, salt, pecans and vanilla. Mix well. Pour into 13x9 baking pan. Cook 25 minutes or, until cake is done. Place small marshmallows on top of hot cake.

FROSTING

1 lb. confectioner's sugar
½ c. whole milk
½ c. cocoa
½ stick margarine

Combine all ingredients and mix until smooth and creamy. Pour over marshmallow cake. After frosting, place whole pecans on top.

Note: If the cake and icing crunch when you bite into it, you've got it right.

Charging the Family Batteries

You never know if you are going to have a short sleeve Thanksgiving or an overcoat Christmas in Greenville. What you could count on is amazing meals and a full table of family.

Thanksgiving was always a special holiday. As the years worn on and the six of us married and began families of our own, one by one we left Greenville for job opportunities. One brother called it following the money. We all called it a time for tough decisions. We would all re-assemble at our parent's bustling home on Main Street for the priority holidays, Thanksgiving and Christmas. For us, it was more than holidays; it was family, filled with rich and entrenched traditions.

With forty-plus to feed, the kitchen was off limits unless you belonged to the team of cooks and helpers, orchestrated by Mom who always had a handle on what was cooking and kept everything orderly with her precise directions of who was to ice the glasses, set the table, take the cornbread out of the oven and the making a meringue for the pies. She left nothing to chance.

Always with perfect timing, we sat at the table at noon. Mom would nod to my oldest brother who fulfilled his tradition to offer up the meal's blessing. After the blessing and as the food was being passed around the table, Dad would acknowledge everyone's presence and ask what's new in each of our lives. Promotions, maybe a move to another city, a baby on the way.

Later in the meal, I remember watching Dad at the head of the table, as he would sit back, deep in his dining room chair and marvel at his six kids and their spouses seated at the adult table. Pride flickered in his eyes. In the kitchen, folding tables were joined together for the kid's table. Mom and Dad would always comment on how big their grandkids were getting, opening the door for eager parents to reveal their kid's latest triumphs.

Half Lebanese and half Scot-Irish were always emphasized by the contents of the special holiday meal. Although, it was never set as a half and half table, we always had a number of Lebanese dishes along with what Mom called Country food.

A large pot of grape leaf rolls sat next to a large bowl of pintos and kibbee next to a baked ham. It truly was the best of both worlds. We fondly called it Mom's Soulful Lebanese. We traced Mom's heritage back to the early 1700s. Her relatives have fought in every American War. Some didn't return home.

Dad's relatives were late comers in comparison, getting here in 1870. Far removed from both sides of the family's origin, all we have kept is the food and a few cuss words. Dad was the first in his family to marry outside of the Lebanese. Their marriage lasted sixty-eight years and resulted in six kids, with eighteen grand kids and 28 great grand kids. No couple in history could have possibly loved each other more. Theirs was a radiating love that we all drew strength from. As second helpings were consumed and bellies poked, nap and football went hand in hand as the kitchen team cleared the table and the kids were sent outside to play.

Later in the day, around dusk, we would start up a caravan of cars and point them towards Deer Creek in Leland, for the light and float show. What an amazing treat! As a kid, I remember how exciting it was. It became even more so to watch our kids marvel at float after float. It was a parade that never moved, but always moving.

Later in the night, kids getting ready for bed, someone would sit at the piano, which always rotated to someone else. The music would go on until the kids were put to bed on a massive pallet; kids, wall to wall. The adult siblings would stay up for hours to reminisce about our younger days and antics we somehow survived. The laughter was deep and sometimes carried tears of joy and aching stomach muscles.

No matter what any of us faced in the crazy and often hectic world beyond Greenville's borders, we always knew we could go home, feel safe and get our human batteries re-charged by plugging into the family energy. We would warm ourselves with memories and love. It was a safe harbor of family and traditions that drew us back every Thanksgiving and Christmas. Short sleeve or overcoat didn't matter.

Family love has no weather gauge.

BLACKBERRY COBBLER

1 pkg. blackberries
2 c. sugar
1 stick butter
1 c. flour
1 c. milk
½ tsp. vanilla

Cook blackberries in 1-cup sugar and water covering berries. Juice will be dark purple. Melt stick of butter in deep baking pan. In separate bowl, mix milk, 1-cup sugar, flour and vanilla. Pour batter over butter in baking dish.

Add blackberries. Do not stir.

Bake in 350* oven, until crust rises to top and browns

Granny Hill

Sitting on her front porch, barefoot, legs dangling and trying to decide if I should eat the apple, the plum or peach first was a tough decision for an eight year old who had just spent the last twenty minutes climbing fruit trees and picking the perfect apple, the best peach and the plumpest plum.

Time stood still at her home. It was quiet, peaceful and always filled with a serenity that in years later would become impossible to find.

To have another twenty minutes of what life was like then would be like grabbing a handful of air or watching water slip between your fingers. It's become a time of memories to treasure.

As I ate the freshly picked fruit she would rock in her wooden, white rocker, hum a church hymn and brush her long gray hair, the longest part danced on the porch floor. A twist, a turn and almost by magic she would mount a bun to the crown of her head and slide in large combs, one on each side, framing her beautiful face. Her paper, church hand-fan stirred the afternoon's humid air.

She didn't sit long. Her hands were too eager to be still. She would leave for a moment and return with a large pan filled to the top with snap beans she had picked just after sunrise that morning, while the heat of the day was still to come.

Her calmness and patience wasn't apparent to me then but she would sit for hours snapping beans, shelling peas or cutting up tomatoes still warm from the vine.

I asked her why she was always working and her answer will stay with me for a lifetime. "Because there's always something to do."

She was a widow that seldom "store bought." She grew her own, canned and froze everything. Waste simply didn't exist, in time or resources. Her small hands were always busy and seemed to know the next step in everything she did.

Filled with fruit from her many, well bearing trees, she offered me an afternoon snack. I knew whatever it was, it would be special and that I would find room for it. I was never disappointed and was soon eating a hot, cathead biscuit bigger than both of my fists, steam waffling up, as the butter melted over the edges and a generous slathering of homemade, best-ever plum jelly crowned the most amazing afternoon treat.

You've heard of women that can take a sack of flour and cook a feast. That was my Granny Hill. Her pleasures were few and simple. Going for a car ride gave her great joy. Stopping at Frostop for a root beer float was a big event even though she lived three blocks from Frostop on Delta Street.
Her world was small and simple. She watched one TV program, "I Love Lucy." Other than that one program, her TV was seldom on.
She had no debt, literally lived off her land and loved life better than anyone I've ever known. She would crochet everything from new baby boots to doilies

and afghans. Her favorite thing to do, and I'm convinced it goes back to her mom and aunts, was making quilts. She and her daughters, (my mom and her sisters) would spend a Saturday, all sitting around a wooden frame, sewing some of the most astounding, beautiful quilts...usually for a family wedding. The joy, laughter and love that went into each quilt, made them priceless family heirlooms.

She wasn't political and was probably not known by a large number of Greenville residents. But in our family she was everything. She lived for others. She gave family love and a moral compass designed from compassion. She was equally loved and cherished in her church family.

Her's was an easy going life that embraced family and church. She would shake her head at today's world driven by technologies, fast food, wastefulness, and crime.

I can still see her sitting in her white, wooden rocker, humming hymns, hands busy, with a peaceful smile and glow of contentment. All that remains of her world are the memories and the way life should be lived.

"There's always something to do."

GRANNY HILL'S CATHEAD BISCUITS

2 c self-rising flour
½ c Crisco
1 c whole milk, cold
3 tbsp. margarine

Blend wet and dry ingredients into a sticky paste.
Spray cookie sheet with Pam.

Spoon dough onto cookie sheet, irregular size.
Lightly coat tops of dough with margarine.

Cook 350* for 20 minutes or until golden brown.

They will rise and have the "appearance" of a cat's head.

Being a Pirate in a Cowboy World

People are amazed when I talk about my hometown of Greenville, Mississippi. They are in awe when I tell them that Greenville hits all the senses. I can see Greenville in my mind's eye. I can smell her aromas; the yacht club, Children's Clinic, Delta Medical Center, Bobby Henry pool, the fresh cut grass on the levee, Doe's just before walking in the door. You could smell Shipley's a block away, Tabb's Bar B Q, Pasquales, Frostop, even Greenville High School had its own smell. All places you can taste, smell, see, hear and feel...and sometimes the feel is way down deep and hangs with a person for a lifetime.

Not even close to the movie version of a kid with a red, Western Flyer wagon, I remember Archie, my resurrected piece-meal wagon. The two front wheels came from a fancy wagon, maybe a Western Flyer. I know its history is grand because the wheels had hub caps. The back two wheels, smaller and from a less grand history, had a flat spot on the left wheel. It limped along like when you have one shoe on.

Archie, had a body made up from an exhausted wooden pallet and would throw out a few splinters if you approached it wrong. What was significant about Archie is, without that crooked, limping wagon I could not have saved money for Boy Scout camp. We would walk the neighborhood, the top of the levee and behind stores on Washington to collect Pepsi and Coke bottles.
Mr. Williams owned William's Grocery, at the corners

of Alexander and Poplar. He was a friendly man that I can't swear to, but believe he overpaid me for the bottles I collected. He knew I was saving up for camp and never tired of seeing me every day for better than two months.

Some days he wouldn't count the bottles but hit a button on his cash register that rang out a bell and he would take money out and hand it to me. Some days he would open the clear, red topped Jack's cookie bin on his wooden counter top and offer me a free cookie. I didn't know it then, but as an adult I understand Mr. Williams. He saw the pirate in me.

Camp day came and I was so excited that the long, hot bus ride didn't bother me. When we passed under the grand Camp Talaha sign, I knew my dreams were coming true. I had set a goal for earning twenty merit badges and had more than enough money left over to buy the sash, at the onsite Boy Scout store. I was pumped when we entered the main activity area and I could see the store and swimming pool.

Scoutmaster Shouffner, told us to change into our bathing suits and go for a swim. We scrambled to the chant; first one in... and was in the pool in minutes, cooling off from the hot bus ride.

The pool was a manmade pool with a sandy bottom. There was an old elephant rope that you could swing out and drop into the murky water. It's not the kind of pool you can see underwater, although I tried. About an hour into the swim I noticed my right eye began to burn. It got worse when the prickly feeling began to swell. It wasn't long before it was so swollen, I couldn't see. I pushed forward, having far too much fun with the troop, daring each other to go further out on the elephant rope.

A friend, I think maybe Kirby, told me I better see about my eye. It looked bad. He called Mr. Shouffner over. I'll never forget the look on my Scoutmaster's face. It was his fear that scared me more than my eye swollen shut. It must have looked pretty rough.

Off to the medic who put drops in my eye and put on a gauze patch. That patch changed my life, forever. Friends I had for years, as far back as I can remember fellow scouts, guys that had shared their inner-most secrets, watched blazing cowboys at the Paramount with, ate ice cream at the Marion Parlor until we got brain-freeze, backed away from me. All of a sudden I had cooties. I was to no small degree, ostracized. Worse than whatever was going on with my eye, I was cut from the herd. I was a pirate in a world of cowboys and Indians.

That week didn't go well. My eye didn't get better and required daily drops and a fresh new eye patch. Close friends were now strangers. Mr. Shouffner knew my goal of twenty merit badges and when I needed a partner to complete the required steps, he was always there for me to bandage for my safety merit badge and he rode with me to get my canoeing merit badge. He saw the pirate in me. I made all twenty merit badges, bought the sash and on the last day of camp, the eye patch was removed.
The memory of being a pirate in a cowboy and Indian world will never go away. That's really what's so special about Greenville. There's a lot of pirates,

some with eye patches, most; without. They are people who are different, cut out of the herd, off of the "norm" scale.

I'm sure every hometown has its people that are different, but what we had was grand people that embraced the least likely...

...the pirates in a world of cowboys and Indians.

It's those people who fight for the underdog. Maybe they were pirates, too. I'm not sure. What I can tell you for sure is they are the builders of character...

....and character is what makes Greenville special.

STUFFED TOMATOES

6-8 large tomatoes
2 c. rice, cooked
1 lb. ground chuck
2 garlic cloves, pound to paste
1 large onion chopped
Dash of cinnamon
½ tsp. salt
1/3 tsp. pepper
1 lb. ground pork
1/3 tsp. allspice

Cut off tops of tomatoes and spoon out. Reserve pulp.
Chop up tomato pulp, add ½ c. water.
Sauté 1 large onion in 1 tbsp. Wesson oil to cook water out of onions.
Add meats and garlic. Cook meat until done, cooking all moisture out of pan by covering and simmering for forty-five minutes   (manually drain)

Add cooked rice to meat mixture. Fill tomatoes. With leftover meat mixture spread in glass casserole dish. Cradle stuffed tomatoes in layer of meat mixture.

Put tomato tops in place on top of filled bottom tomatoes.

Bake 25 minutes at 350*. Do not cover.

Hurricanes and Tornadoes

You can take the boy out of the Delta but.....

I can remember terrible storms blowing up out of nowhere. We kids were herded into the bathroom in the middle of the house and made to stay there until the tornado winds calmed. I clearly remember some scary times being hidden away in the center of the house, wind howling and heavy rains beating on the roof. But the worst of it all was when it got real quiet. That's when you wonder. That's when fear taps you on the shoulder.

Coming from a land-locked community and then living ocean side, seven-hundred and fifty miles off the US coast could be a bit daunting. Islanders called it Rock Fever. Not once did I ever feel confined or removed from the world. I loved every minute, well except for that time, I rode out my first hurricane. Folks in Florida have hurricane parties. How bad can it be?

The back wall was all glass and overlooked the amazing ocean. What an astounding view! The view was why Carol and I selected that house on the Ocean. We watched massive ocean liners pass right by our patio. We could take a few steps toss in a fishing line and catch a shark or a tuna.

Really. Jason was fourteen the first time he caught a shark. He got it up to the shore and we were grilling not an hour later. I knew no one would believe him, or me for that matter, so out comes the trusty camera...captured for the naysayers and doubters. Grilled shark is the bomb. Grilled tuna, even better.

The week-end a hurricane was forecast. I sent Carol and Jason stateside. I stayed with the house and my job.

Standing at that beautiful glass wall, I watched and marveled at nature and her fury. Forty mile an hour wind...how bad can it get? I watched the palm trees sway and what a sight! Fascinating! The waves were tall and angry lapping at the shore, at least what I could still see was left of the shoreline. I think the island got a little smaller, gobbled up by massive waves.

In the wee hours I found what I thought was the center of the house, made a pallet and settled in for the night. The wind worsened, so I drew the blanket closer and was actually okay with it all. Palm trees toppling over, stuff flying through the air, I felt safe, knowing I had claimed the safest spot in the house. Folks from the South know what to do in nasty winds.

I think what spooked me was the all-glass back wall. I had never heard glass BEND. Yep, that's right, that stuff bends under heavy winds and has the most eerie sound, similar to a fingernail down a chalkboard, only much worse and with consequences. It was the proverbial shoe waiting to drop.

For the first time, fear tapped me on the shoulder. I moved to inside the center bathroom. The idea of all of that glass breaking with me in the line of fire... But I was safe, my Greenville experience with tornadoes had prepared me.

Around four that morning, my neighbor, a lifetime citizen of Bermuda called me. How odd, phone ringing at four am, during the peak winds now bumping better than eighty-five miles an hour...which of course, I didn't know were amplified if you live on the ocean front. There's nothing to obstruct the winds. Sometimes we learn pertinent information on the fly and maybe a bit too late.

Red, my neighbor asked how I was holding up. I told him fine, no problems. I watched the storm, read some in my book and had camped out in the center of the house and was riding out the hurricane fine....Thanks for asking. Southerners know about high winds.

"Oh My God! You didn't go to the center of the house!"

"Well, yes. That's the safest place."

"No, you aren't in the Mississippi Delta, my friend. The Bermuda homes are made with concrete slate roofs. They CAVE IN at the CENTER of the house during a hurricane!"

I promised myself I would never, ever ride out another hurricane.

PICKLED GREEN TOMATOES

Small firm green tomatoes
1 stalk celery
1sweet green peppers
5 peeled garlic pods
2 qt. Water
1 qt. Vinegar

Pack small tomatoes in sterilized quart jars.

Add to each quart: 1 bud of peeled garlic, 1 stalk cut up celery, 1 sweet pepper, cut into ¼ inch slices.

Make brine from water and vinegar and salt.
Cook brine for 5 minutes.

Pour brine over tomatoes and seal at once.

Ready to eat in 4 to 6 weeks.

Death of a Legend

I had to get my legs back under me before I could react. It's a lot to absorb that Shine was beaten and killed. My prayers, thoughts and condolences to Shine's family and friends with a farewell salute to a kind and gentle soul that made every trip to Greenville a highlight.

When we visited my parents in Greenville, we always stopped to visit Shine and of course stock up on his wonderful tamales. He always greeted us with his trademark smile and without fail would ask how my dad was doing. They were friends for many decades.

Dad knew when we left his home and were headed back, we would always on the way out of town, stop at Shines. Dad would wave goodbye to us and say, "Tell Shine hello, for me."

It was our tradition. Something we looked forward to. A visit with Shine completed our Greenville visit. I can't say the three hour drive smelling Shine's tamales was easy. I can't recall how many times we pulled over on the shoulder of the road and ate a few tamales, on the run.

When we lived in Bermuda, we always stocked up on Shine's tamales and took a lot of them back to Bermuda with us. Shine always had a story about some "stuff" that he and dad had gotten into in their earlier years. His stories were always funny and often had some moral lesson tucked neatly away.

Getting on the small airplane from Greenville to Memphis, not much bigger than the can that held the tamales, drove every passenger on board nuts, asking what is that wonderful smell? I would slide the tamales deeper under the seat, but there was no escaping that incredible aroma.

When we arrived in Bermuda, there was always a group of friends waiting to dive into Shine's tamales. When I told Shine that he was internationally known and loved, he would smile and say, "I know."

After losing both parents, our trips back to Greenville were less often, but when we did go home, we kept our tradition of stopping by to visit with Shine, stock up on his tamales and listen to his warming stories about his and my dad's younger days. What those thugs, those nasty animals took from us was far more than the few dollars they stole from Shine. They took the last of our tradition. There is no way for those ignorant, backwards, low-life scum to know that they stole one of Greenville's treasures.

Rest well, Shine. Justice will be done.

When you see my dad, tell him I said hello.

ITALIAN CREAM CAKE

1 stick Parkay
½ c. oil
2 c. sugar
5 egg yolks
2 c. self-rising flour
5 egg whites
1 tsp. baking soda
1 c. buttermilk
1 tsp. vanilla
1 c. coconut
1 c. chopped pecans

Cream butter and oil: add sugar. Beat until smooth. Add egg yolks and beat well.

Combine flour and baking soda: add to creamed mixture. Alternating buttermilk into mixture. (Some flour, then some buttermilk and so on.)

Stir in vanilla, coconut and pecans. Fold in egg whites and beat well. Pour into 3 greased cake pans or 1 large sheet cake pan.

Bake at 350* for 35 minutes or until toothpick can be pulled out clean.

ICING

8 oz. cream cheese
½ stick Parkay
1-box confectioner's sugar
1 tsp. vanilla
1 c. chopped nuts
1 c. coconut

Beat cheese and butter smooth: add sugar and mix well. Add vanilla and beat until smooth. Add nuts and coconut. Spread on cooled cake.

Note: this is one of many cakes Mom baked every Christmas.

Seeing the World at Age Eleven

There's a time and place in every young boy's heart that he dreams of a bicycle that will defeat the wind and overcome gravity. I clearly remember the day my dream came true. I was celebrating my eleventh birthday and the absolute ultimate surprise was from my parents.

Knowing we didn't have a lot of money and knowing the cost of a new bike would restrict my parent's ability to feed eight people, I was fully open to the refurbished bike from Jones Gun shop.

It didn't matter to me that some boy had used the new off. I had the best part of here and now. I was fairly used to hand-me-down clothes and was grateful for whatever I got. It's that way in a big family. You don't always get to wear off the new, and that's okay. It's the getting that counts. It's the loving parents that are doing their best to open as many doors as they can for a small army of kids with diverse wants and needs.

I remember one Christmas my brother begged, literally begged for a chemistry set. I can still see his wide eyes and shaking hands when he opened a chemistry set that Christmas morning. Little, did we know, that in a few months he would almost burn our home down with his concoctions. Sometimes dreams can backfire or at the very least have consequences...which brings us back to my first bike. We lived next to the levee. It was our playground.

Now when you mount a dream, literally and point it down the dirt road on top of the levee to see what's down that road...there are consequences.

In my pursuit to "see the world" beyond my parents parameters, I peddled that bike for all she was worth. Free to roam the levee, I explored cattle, saw a few snakes and could see for miles and all the lush greenery beyond the bottom of the levee and main roads filled with cars. It was new to me and an awesome sight.

The bike didn't come with a watch, nor did it have an odometer. What it did have, was a free spinning pedal action that I loved. The wind rushing against my face and the power to move me and that bike a sizable distance. I didn't realize it at the time, but the distance I had traveled, was an equal distance to get back home.

There's a lesson in here that has kept me from doing such a foolish thing again. I peddled hard and fast trying to beat the sunset, which was my curfew. I knew if I wasn't home by dark there would be a strong disciplinarian waiting for me and that involved a heated, no a scorching of the bottom side.

Pump as I might, push as hard as I could, I had ventured out far too far to meet curfew and I suppose it should be no surprise that my legs ached enough that it blurred my vision. Add in the anticipation of a spanking for breaking curfew, and my dear friend I was in a world of hurt. I pushed harder, faster and tried to ignore the pains shooting through my legs. It was an eternity before I began recognizing familiar ground and knew I was getting close.

Then, I was faced with a new dilemma. Well into dark and certainly well beyond curfew, I questioned if there were a real hurry for what was waiting for me. I rested at the top of the levee, looking at my home, lit up in the night, knowing what was to come. I distinctly remember my butt heating up in anticipation. I loved my bike and knew that would be part of the discipline. No more bike riding for a long time.

I drew in a long breath, rode that bucking bronco down the levee to the side yard and parked it. I took a moment to admire it, knowing we would be separated in a matter of moments.

When I entered our home, my brothers and sisters were all huddled around the white glow TV set. Mom or Dad weren't home. My sister called me to the kitchen and set out a plate for me. That's something that is never done. If you aren't there at supper time, you didn't eat. Pretty simple, hard-fast rule. She sat with me while I ate and told me mom and dad had gone to the picture show. I wondered if she would tell on me when they got home.

She never did. Nor did any of my siblings. I grew a different respect for my sisters and brothers, that day. I escaped the discipline, but have since lived the lesson, over and over.

Measure twice, cut once.

Ironing in the Snow

Southerners as a rule aren't worth their salt and will do whatever is necessary to avoid a good snow. If it means parking the four wheeler, storing the truck in the garage and watching out the window for good ole Mississippi gumbo to re-appear.

In the first few minutes, as snow begins to fall, tongues will dart out for a taste. Some will pull the top off the garbage cans for a makeshift sled. The levee will be covered with people you have never seen before. Give them about twenty minutes, their toes will get brittle, earlobes fall off and they'll find them a window to watch for gumbo to return.

At our house, Mom would send us out to get the top snow so she could make us a rare winter time treat, snow creme. One year some news reporter said that the snow had nuclear waste in it and advised everyone to not eat it. We laughed at the reporter and had our fill of snow creme. None of us glowed.

Dad was at work and Mom had joined all the other moms at the grocery store. She wanted to be sure we had enough to get us through the slow-down, which usually meant even the grocery stores closed. They just as well close, there wasn't much left on the shelves.

My brother, the genius, had a great idea. Mom had a brand new metal ironing board. Back then a guy's crease in his pants was everything. It told the world if he was civil or a slob. Thinking ourselves at least somewhat civil, we opted for the pant-crease. Actually, it was Mom who had determined that her tribe would be civil. I'm not so sure if she hadn't pressed the issue...and our pants, us kids would have opted for the easy way, and lived a wrinkled life.

My brother stood on the metal ironing board, grabbed the pointed nose end and pulled up, bending it to make it more aerodynamic. He got the first ride from the top of the levee and I can't remember seeing anyone go that fast that wasn't in a car. I couldn't wait for my turn.

Being the runt of the litter and terribly thin, my brother decided it wouldn't be safe for me to go alone, so I piled on with him and off we went. I could hear the snow crunching underneath us as my eyes teared from the bitter cold wind, whooshing by, going faster and faster. I can only guess that my brother never thought the cross telephone poles at the bottom of the levee would be an obstacle. Each telephone pole set lengthwise had cut off poles on each end about two feet high, just high enough that lawn mowers could get under them to keep the grass at bay.

They were there to stop cars from driving up the levee, not stop some kids on a homemade sled. Surely we wouldn't go that far, but here they come, and moving at us at a fast clip. My brother yelled, "Duck" as we both leaned forward and pulled our bodies down as close to the ground as we could.

We thought we were okay as we cleared underneath the telephone poles, but that became a past problem with one major problem still in front of us. We had momentum, no brakes, packed so tight on the upside down ironing board we couldn't bail out, and we were headed for oncoming traffic.

There is no such thing as a Southerner that can drive in snow. Some may brag about it and go faster than everyone else in their Bubba fashion, but the fact is, Southerners are helpless in snow.

The one car headed straight for us, swerved, slid in the snow and came to a skidding stop. We didn't. We kept going for almost another block. Zipping by the car like we had some fire to go to. When we finally stopped, my brother was laughing so hard, he couldn't stop. That's how he deals with shock. He laughs...almost howls, at what could have been. The laughing stopped when an arm snatched my brother off the sled, pulling the bottom half of me with him. That car? That one and only car....it was our Dad! And he wasn't laughing. My rear began to burn. I knew what was coming. One thing I can say about my brother, he has a silver tongue. He stated his case, about you won't believe how fast that ironing board will travel down the levee.

The next thing I knew, we were at the top of the levee, moved down away from the telephone poles and my Dad was on that flipped over ironing board, literally flying down the levee. I realized that day how good it is for kids to see their parents laugh.

We spent the afternoon riding that ironing board for all it was worth, which was seven dollars and some change. We had to collect bottles, cut yards with a push mower and had a list two miles long of household chores to replace Mom's new ironing board. To this day, when it snows, I go looking for a metal ironing board.

Sometimes, Mississippi gumbo ain't so bad.

PEACH COBBLER

1 large can peaches
1 stick butter
1 c. sugar
1 c. milk
1 c. flour
½ tsp. vanilla flavoring
Dash cinnamon
Dash allspice

Put butter in large casserole dish.
Microwave one minute to melt butter.
Mix together sugar, flour, milk, vanilla flavoring, and spices.
Pour mixture over butter.
Pour peaches with can juice on top. Do not stir.
Cook in oven 350* for forty minutes to an hour, to golden top crust.

The Delta Blues

If I had a time machine and could go back and alter only one thing for Greenville; I would set the time for 1962 and open up a free, state of the art recording studio. Much like the 1940s and 50s, Greenville was a mecca for literati. She became the place to be for both accomplished and aspiring writers. The shining age of Greenville's literati began fading in the late fifties and a recording studio would have been timely to replace the loss of not only the literati world but the devastating loss of the U.S. Air Force base. Both brought Greenville to her knees in their painful exits.

While Greenville had more than her share of gifted writers, she also had an over-abundance of creative, edgy musicians that ultimately faded into the shadows of almost, because they had little to no opportunity of capturing and covering the world with their distinct, Mississippi Delta, vibrant music.

Some local musicians broke through and some with astounding success, like Bruce Blackman and other major notables. Certainly not to take away from their success, but there were hundreds of musicians, uniquely talented that could have been international successes had we only known, gave them the forum and let destiny take the driver's wheel.

I may be wrong and I am totally committed; right or wrong, but I believe the face of Greenville would be completely different today, had we only given so many with astounding talent a place in the sun, if only for a moment. Today, we know the key to music is first talent, which we obviously had ample, followed by distribution...which was and probably remains to be today, the ultimate factor of success or failure.

RCA distribution ended up ripping off Stax and owning most of her original music. Stax in turn, ripped off far too many musicians to mention. It was and is a vicious business filled with greed, theft and corruption.

Our Greenville studio would have been staffed with interactive, skillful attorneys that would protect the artists, their properties and their royalties with only the best agreements for distribution. Based on that one recording studio, Greenville musicians would have been sent on tour, all over the world to promote their records. Fame and fortune would have been theirs and Greenville would have taken her rightful place in music history.

We could have, should have, become the mecca for bright, new and innovative musicians that today have thousands of written pages of unrecorded music collecting dust in the attics of what could have been. It's like having a three year old playing Mozart. If he isn't nurtured, in time he will end up at some piano bar playing "Tie a Yellow Ribbon." My time machine would alter opportunities. The tattered, yellowed pages of music that remain collecting dust, would have changed the world of music and gave Greenville's amazing musicians their due.

Why must hindsight always be 100%?

COCONUT PIE

5 Tbsp. flour
1 tsp. vanilla
2 c. milk
2 eggs, separated
1 pkg. coconut
1 pie shell
5 tbsp. sugar
Dash of salt

Put flour in saucepan: add sugar, salt and milk.
Cook on low heat until mixture begins to thicken.
Take a little of the flour mixture and put in a bowl with egg yolks, stir well.
Pour into saucepan.
Continue cooking until mixture is thick.
Just before taking from heat, add coconut and vanilla.
In a separate bowl, beat egg whites with 2 tablespoons of sugar.
Then add 2 more tablespoons of sugar and beat.
Add ½ teaspoon of vanilla.
When thick and fluffy, put meringue on top of pie and bake until lightly brown. (3-5 minutes).

Note: Mom always sprinkled a little coconut on top of meringue before baking.

SOUTH PAW

There was a time and place I could show my age by putting up my left and right hand. Mrs. Black at Susie P. Trigg taught fourth grade and was the first and only teacher I've ever had that was naturally left handed.

When she noticed that my handwriting was, let's say, sub-par, she told me that when she was a child the adults tied her left hand behind her back and forced her to write with her right hand. Stuttering and nightmares followed.

Until I walked in her class, I couldn't write worth diddly. It wasn't from lack of trying. All right handed teachers taught right handed and couldn't relate to writing "backwards."

I became her "project" and in short order she had me writing to a level that was actually recognizable. Her detailed and careful instructions have stayed with me for a lifetime. She had an impact that no other teacher had.

I learned to use both hands, not just to tell my age, but when called on, I can use my right hand almost as well as my left...favoring the left.

Like she told me, "It's a maddening world out there. You have to adapt."

Thank you, Mrs. Black.

WHITE COCONUT CAKE

1 Duncan Hines butter recipe yellow cake mix.
Bake by box directions.

ICING

2 eggs, separated
1 c. sugar
¼ c. water
Dash of salt
1/3 c. white karo syrup
1 tsp. vanilla

Whip 2 egg whites in bowl.
In saucepan, cook sugar, water, salt and karo syrup until it strings.
Slowly add mixture to the beaten egg whites with blender on low.
Continue to beat until thick.
Add vanilla and blend.
Put icing on cake and sprinkle top and sides with coconut, covering the entire cake.

Boat Building 101

Every guy should have a friend like Bob. Whenever I'd have a hair brain idea, Bob's reaction was always the same. "Giddy up."

One of my brothers, an avid duck hunter, called me over to show me his newest project. I was smitten and on fire to get started. He had taken one sheet of plywood, a few 2x2s, a lot of spit and glue and had built a duck blind boat. I saw the possibilities way beyond duck blind. I left with the homemade template drawn out on old newspapers.

I called Bob. The next morning my driveway had saw horses, plywood, 2x2s, water sealer, fiberglass, tape and a whole lot of energy to burn. I played out my ideas to Bob. "Giddy up."

The dumb idea of attaching a trolling motor to this thing not much bigger than a toy has to go down in the book of idiots, page one. Closely followed by, would you really want a boat that you can lift over your head with one hand?

Picture a snubbed nose and blunt tail kayak. The boat literally couldn't hold a person and a laugh at the same time.

I told Bob, that every good fisherman knows the fish are always on bank on the "other" side. We'd have to cross Lake Washington. "Giddy up."
Bologna sandwich in one hand, steering the trolling motor with the other, we were Masters of the

Universe, Kings of the waterway. Bob in his boat, me in mine.
It didn't seem that far...

The early morning fishing was amazing and promised a fish fry for plenty. Then around nine am, a few dark clouds started gathering and enough wind that it was difficult to untie the yo-yos. Double disk, much like a kid's yoyo with a line and hook. (When the bait and hook are nibbled by a fish it triggers the yoyo to retract with a zip, hooking and pulling the fish up out of the water.)

The wind got stronger. That's when I started cutting down the yo-yos and found my hurry up. I shouted out to Bob we need to head back to shore. "Giddy up."

I was four steps behind Mother Nature.

There's white caps lapping and entering the, "almost a good idea" boats. Of the three foot white caps, two and a half feet was when we were in the down swell. It's bad.

We aren't going to make it. We're literally in the middle of Lake Washington, in boats that should be in some kid's bathtub, with waves lapping in, on both sides, wind howling, raining so hard that there's as much water above as there is below...and the one speed trolling motors are as useless as one of them things on a boar hog.

I hollered over to Bob to pull out his paddle and give it all he's got. "Giddy up."

We strained against wind, rain and waves, motor puttering and the J-stroke we learned at Camp Tallaha got us moving, but barely. Then it happened! The sky went blue, no wind, no rain, and no more white caps, smooth as glass.

When we got back to the shore, we both spent a few minutes on our knees. I'm not sure if Bob was praying or resting, but my knee-time wasn't spent resting.

I looked over at Bob and said,
"We made a mistake...we should have went to Lake Lee."

"Giddy up."

FRIED APPLE OR PEACH PIES

FILLING

6 oz. dried apples or peaches
½ c. water
1/3 c. sugar

Fruit and water in saucepan cook covered on low for
45 minutes.
Stir in sugar. Prepare dough as below.

FRIED PIE DOUGH

2 c. self-rising flour
¼ c. shortening
¾ c. milk

Pour flour in a small mixing bowl. Cut in shortening
with fork. Stir in milk. Mix dough to no longer sticky.
Heat up ½ cup Wesson oil in large frying fan.

Pinch off dough and make a ball the size of a small
egg.
Sprinkle with flour and roll thin and flat into a 5 inch
circle.
Place 2 tbsp. of fruit on bottom half of dough.
Fold top over to meet bottom. Press edges with fork.
Prick pie in 3-4 places to vent while cooking.

Place in hot grease and fry on both sides until golden brown.

Best served hot. I can smell them cooking.

Break out the ice cream!

LEMON POUND CAKE

1 pkg. Duncan Hines lemon cake mix
1/3 c. Wesson oil
1 c. water
1 pkg. lemon instant pudding mix (4 serving size)
4 eggs

Preheat oven to 350* generously grease and flour
bunt cake pan. Blend all ingredients in a large mixing
bowl. Beat for 2 minutes at medium speed. Bake 50
minutes or by toothpick test. Cool 25 minutes before
adding glaze.

GLAZE

Blend 1 c. confectioner's sugar with 2 tbsp. milk using
blender until smooth.
Be sure you've allowed cake to cool at least 25
minutes.
Drizzle glaze over cake.

When White Tail Deer Laugh

There are two kinds of hunters in the Mississippi Delta; guest or member. If you are a guest, you aren't going to hunt much. It's an honor to be invited but the invite list is short and the guest list is as long as Herman Solomon's arm down an E.E. Bass, crowded hallway after the last bell had rung.

There's two kinds of hunting clubs; one that everyone else belongs to that actually IS a hunting club... and then there's Chisolm.

The Mississippi Indians limped away from the small island, vowing to never return. The Chickasaw and Choctaw would never chance looking straight-on at the island in daylight. I never, not for a moment, believed the rumor that Chisolm's impossible terrain was used to train our military elite, only to abort the exercise.

Funny how things are so shiny and bright in the beginning but when you look back later, everything that whispered yes was no more than the foul breath of the Devil, himself.

Chisolm, of course, is the hunting club Bob and I joined. Bob was all-in with his hearty, "Giddy up." No more begging for a guest invite. We were now proud owners of a membership and could hunt when we wanted. Membership has its privileges and that meant bragging rights. We figured jealous non-members was the cause of laughter when we proudly displayed our member pin.

No one bothered to tell us that we had become members to the only place on earth that took in more members than gave back. If we had known, we could have checked the daily member sign-in sheets. We discovered later, much too late, the sign-ins were plenty and the sign outs were few. It should have been our first warning.

Anyone that has spent three days or more in the Delta knows what gumbo is - and it ain't the eating kind like south of us. What most are not familiar with is Chisolm gumbo. It's the boot sucking kind of gumbo that can lock you down for hours...depending on the last time it rained.

That's how we spent our first day hunting on Chisolm. Locked down, near knee deep in a swamp-like Chislom gumbo that we both swore was quicksand. The harder we fought to get loose, the deeper we sank. Deer ran by laughing their white tails off.

Exhausted after a half day of fighting Chisolm gumbo, we did the absolute unthinkable. We set up camp. We didn't know that any intelligent person dared not sleep on the island. It's just unheard of....ask our military elite. They had to call in the helicopters to extract the tactical team.

Tent stakes are a simple matter. You hammer them into the ground and they do their job of holding up the tent. Not on Chisolm. The gumbo that sucked the boots right off our feet, wouldn't hold a tent steak. Water bubbled up around the tent steaks and they would ooze out and flop on the ground, flat. Useless. We ended up tying rope off to nearby trees for the tent to stay in a full and upright position. More deer walked by, laughing their white tails off at us.

I can't say we slept that night, for all the deer coming by and laughing at us. I'm fairly sure they all brought their relatives by to see what we look like.

Mosquitoes the size of bumble bees kept us busy slapping and groaning. We didn't bother with a campfire and opted for a can of vienna sausage inside the tent. We had to share our dinner with the uninvited mosquitoes.

I remember wondering if daylight would ever come...and if it does; could we ever find our way out?

Look before you buy.

Giddy up.

SOCK IT TO ME CAKE

1 pkg. Duncan Hines butter recipe golden cake mix
1 c. (8oz) dairy sour cream
1/3 c. Wesson oil
¼ c. sugar
¼ c. water.
4 eggs
2 tbsp. reserved cake mix
1 c. finely chopped pecans
2 tsp. cinnamon
2 tsp. brown sugar

Combine filling ingredients and set aside. In a large mixing bowl blend on medium speed: cake mix, sour cream, oil, ¼ c. sugar water and eggs. Beat at high speed for 2 minutes once all ingredients are added. Pour 2/3 of the batter into a greased and floured pan. Sprinkle filling ingredients evenly over batter in pan. Spread remaining batter over filling mixture. Bake 375* for 45-50 minutes. Cool in pan 25 minutes, then remove from pan.

GLAZE

1 c. confectioner's sugar blended with 2 tbsp. milk with blender on medium speed. Allow cake to cool 25 minutes before drizzling glaze over cake.

The Soul of Growing Up

It was the summer of 1962. I was fourteen years old had earned my Star rank in the Boy Scouts and was soon headed for Camp Tallaha to begin my quest for Life rank, with Eagle in my sights. Things in my life had begun to change. Scouting was losing the shine off its bumpers and the females, all of a sudden, became beautiful and had lost their cooties.

To be at that age and have an older brother ask if you wanted to "go riding" wasn't just a thrill, it was a first step into manhood. Going for a ride meant slowly, almost creeping through Stazi's, then to Dan's Bar B Q, a circle drive off Walnut, up the levee, a few short ups and downs of the sharp incline, at top of the wharf, then onto Central Street, and back to Stazi's, then Dan's and so on to finish the nightly loop, only to repeat it, again and again.

The sun had set and the day began to cool. We had made five, maybe six loops, stopped for a cherry coke at Stazi's and my brother for some unexplained reason broke the cycle and turned onto Highway One, North.

Part of the drive was familiar, at least to around Bing's Grocery store. After that, it was new territory to me and obviously very familiar to him. He pulled into a large gravel parking lot that was near filled to capacity. There was a muffled sound coming from a large white building and I remember my brother's hand tapping out the music he was hearing coming out of that old building. I heard muffled, he heard every note.

We cruised the lot, looking for a parking spot and found one close to the main door.

"I got to go in and see a guy. You sit here and wait. I won't be long."

Proud to be along for the ride, I agreed. He disappeared inside and my eyes wandered looking the place over. A large painted sign above the door read, VFW.

I thought that odd since my Uncle worked at the VFW and this wasn't where he worked.

A black guy came out of the front door and left it standing wide open. It was then I could clearly hear the music and an incredible singer...and maybe, I wasn't sure at the moment but I think the piano was real familiar.

Second, maybe third song, there was no doubt. I didn't recognize anyone or any other instrument, but all doubts went away on the sound of the piano. That...was my brother!

Another patron exited the front door and it closed. The music became muffled. I strained to hear and another black guy exited, leaving the door open, again.
The most amazing singer was pulling his heart out of his chest and handing it to everyone within earshot. He was amazing. I was tempted to go inside, but I

knew if I did, I may not get invited to "go riding" again. So, I sat and listened to some of the most incredible music I've ever heard. It was life-changing music.

About forty-five minutes later my brother returned to the car and we left.
We both sat quiet until we were close to Dan's Bar B Q and I broke the silence and asked him why that sign read VFW, when we both knew the VFW was out by the Country Club.

"That was the black VFW." He answered.

"Oh. Who was that singing?" I asked.

"Otis Redding... "

Pass the Tamales

Nothing smacks of Greenville and the Mississippi Delta better than her distinct food. At the top of that food list would be hot tamales.

Dad would make a tamale run to Doe's and pick up dozens of tamales in a large metal can filled with tamale juice that would make you kiss your fingers. His next stop was Brown's for the fresh, bite the air, french bread and his final stop was Shipley's for plain, glazed donuts. It was an occasion, an event that followed second to Christmas.

It didn't happen often. Money was tight and such an event was at that time considered an extravagant meal. The semi-rare, mouth-watering anticipation was amazing.

In the years that followed and "eating out" became more readily available, we kept the tamale tradition almost on sacred ground. That is, we didn't allow the cherished event to become a McDonald's experience. McTamales.

When Doe's did the unthinkable and began wrapping tamales in paper, the magic was lost but only for a moment. Enter....Shine. Our tradition now fully restored and wrapped in shucks, we transferred all of our tamale orders to Shine. We were so accustomed to "sucking the shuck" and delighting in that aroma and taste. Sorry about that Doe's, but we were stuck on shucks!

Now in Doe's favor, we continued eating their mouthwatering steaks and eventually the tamales again. They are, of course, delicious - paper or shucks.

A few years back, I was driving through Bull Frog Corner (yes, that's a major intersection in Southaven), and noticed a familiar sign on a store front. It was so familiar, so intensely mouthwatering that I crossed over four lanes of heavy, unforgiving traffic to pull in to the new business. My wife, of course, thought I had finally lost my mind, until she saw the familiar sign. We didn't talk. We scrambled out of the car and dashed inside, laughing like kids.

It was Shipley's Donuts. I ordered a practice run of a dozen donuts. At first sight and during the first bite, and the intoxicating smell, I was seven years old again and wondered if anyone noticed I was now wearing a Roy Rogers t- shirt, shorts and was barefoot, toes spreading a-part in sheer delight. My brain and my tongue agreed it was 1955 and the only thing that could possibly improve the moment was a glass of ice cold milk from a glass bottle.

My eyes rolling back in my head in a clash of then and now when I noticed on their menu board that they have hot tamales. No trial run....I ordered three dozen. With a brain now pitched into high gear, I wondered where I could get a fresh loaf of french bread. Wal Mart, just down the street bakes bread, daily. One more stop to complete the jog down memory lane. I ordered two more dozen donuts.

It's not Greenville's own, well, yes it is. Actually the owner, a close friend of the McGaugh family, opened his Southaven Shipley shop and the first thing he did was hire a guy in Greenville to make tamales for his Shipley franchise. On a scale of one to ten, I'd rate the tamales in shucks, at an even ten.

Carol and I had tamales and laughed, french bread and smiled and Shipley's donuts, the ultimate for dessert, last night. It's no longer a three hour drive, but only ten minutes from our Southaven home. No time machine could go any faster.

The next time, I brought in a container for tamale juice, the Shipley employee, a life time Southaven resident, asked me if I was from Greenville. Apparently it's a Greenville tradition to bring your own juice container. I'm sure she has heard plenty of Greenville stories.

It's apparent I was a bit slow discovering a part of the Mississippi Delta, moved to Southaven. Seems a lot of former Greenville residents have discovered a slice of back home and keep the tamale juice ladle busy.

A slice of back home.

Blow Hard Pecans

If there was a blow-hard storm, we knew it meant getting up early...like daylight early. Mom gave each of us a neatly folded Kroger brown paper bag and sent us on our way. Between our home and the Taggart's home on Poplar Street, there was a huge pecan tree that hung over the street. The hurry was to get to the fallen pecans before traffic flattened them out. Our small army would race and compete to see who could pick up the most, the fastest, flagging any early cars around a street full of freshly fallen pecans.

Storms back then were violent with heavy winds and silver dollar sized raindrops. It was years later that I witnessed my first rain-mist and the sun was out. A true sign the devil was beating his wife. Gave me the willies. Sort of like a cat barking.

We would hold off the traffic and pick up as many pecans as we could until the traffic became so heavy, we had to relinquish the road to the cars.

Back home, the room was full of laughter, with one liners, wise cracks and giggles as we laid out newspapers on the floor, each with our own brick for a foundation and a hammer or something close to a hammer and the cracking would begin. After all the smashing, whole pecans were something of a novelty and revered enough that they had their own bowl. We peeled pecans and filled bowls mostly of pieces that survived the brick.

In the teamwork we knew that Mom would be baking

pecan pies and my personal favorite, a white coconut cake, filled with pecans. Sometimes the honored whole pecans graced the top of the cake. Every Thanksgiving and Christmas we saw our reward for rising early, gathering pecans and those funny moments of siblings working together in the midst of humor and smashing brick to brick.

I remember years later looking up the definition of pecan. Old man Webster must have been watching us kids because he defines pecan as "a nut cracked by a stone." Give that man a slice of pecan pie.

It's said that a lot of what we are is attributed to DNA. I'm proof of it. My Dad was a sucker for every gadget, gizmo and new fangled thing promising to make life better.

He bought and we tried every pecan breaker from commercially produced to hand made in some guy's garage that assured us of obtaining the illusive whole pecan. I am still in search of the ideal pecan cracker, buying every new swing around, fool proof, best ever, and most improved pecan breaker invented.

The violent storms that brought us pecans, the times of siblings sitting Indian style working in harmony and humor and the smell of Mom's kitchen are all neatly tied to a simple, nature provided treat that bears…

… **the life lesson of working for what you want.**

Christmas Memories

The smell of a live Christmas tree brings back great memories. Bubbling lights, flashing and flickering, and each special decoration that comes with its own story. The frail Belgium hand blown figures, the plastic elves that scream 1940 and the whiskered Santa-heads that light up the tree.

Garlands bring back a time when popcorn was strung and wrapped round and round the tree. Long plastic ice icicles and the aluminum-like icicles carefully hung one at a time. But then I'm getting ahead of myself.

First, you had to pick out the perfect, full and well-shaped tree. Then getting it home atop the car, roped in better than any calf at a rodeo. The huge metal stand and the trunk had to match which meant sawing to the lengths of aching arms to get the base of the tree to fit in the metal stand. The fresh smell of pine filled our home.

Once the tree is secure in its stand, then testing the lights before hanging on the tree usually meant replacing the large bright colored bulbs. Then there was the challenge to make sure that when you get to the last string of lights that you had the male end to plug into the wall.

If you ever got them backwards and ended up with a female end and no way to plug the lights into the wall outlet; well, you didn't make that mistake twice. Then you have to have it right at the top, too...so you will have a male and female to connect the treetop angel's lights.

When my two sisters were small kids, maybe seven or eight, they pooled their long-saved monies together and went to Ben Franklin's on Washington Avenue and bought a rather plain but beautiful angel. She didn't have lights and in her simplistic way became the crown atop our family Christmas tree for decades. The lighted angel came when the simplistic angel began showing her age and was ceremoniously retired. She now resides in a glass case in my sister's home, after our oldest sister lost her valiant battle with cancer.

For years, they passed that angel back and forth, each keeping her for a year. The plain angel was as much a part of Christmas as the tree. Retiring her was a hard decision. Her back story of two kids saving their dimes and pooling their money to buy that angel made her that much more special to our family.

I suppose some would have trouble understanding the personal attachments to the special dime store angel, as well as the fondness towards individual decorations, but the five plastic, very red Santa's with a huge smile, white lined suit, and black boots or the reindeer decorations had been on the family Christmas tree before memories began for most of us.

They were handpicked by our parents and were far more special than the ordinary ornaments you buy today, usually stamped "Made in China." Glass globes are very fragile and carefully stored away at the end of each Christmas. The fact that they didn't get bumped and smash to the floor each year was amazing.

Although, some did end up in hundreds of shards on the floor. Maybe because most of the decorations were fragile and survived for so many years made them special...or maybe because we had grown accustomed to each one and looked for those extra special ornaments hanging somewhere on the tree. The family tradition that each family member would hang at least one ornament on the tree, remains today. Everybody participated.

Whatever the attachment we all had for the real tree, the plain angel and each ornament, why we all rejoiced in each year's tree and seeing the ornaments resting in boxes, soon to be hung on the tree I can't put a finger on. Maybe it was the safety of knowing they were always there. Maybe we were happily stuck in years past and liked being stuck there.

What I can tell you is, things change. The frail and fragile ornaments over the years, no matter the care applied will be broken. There will be less and less each year.

I remember the year the large Christmas lights were swapped out for the more modern, small lights. When one went out on the new string of lights, the whole line went dark. That never happened with the big lights. One of the big boys burnt out, you simply replaced that one light bulb. The changing of the lights from old to modern was only a small sign of what was to come. Losing the bubbling lights in exchange for the newer smaller lights never did settle well. I still miss those silly, bubbling lights.

One Christmas new ornaments were bought to replace all of the broken and worn ornaments that we knew and expected to see on the tree. I can't say it was pandemonium, but I can say it was different. One of those differences you notice, are effected by but don't speak of. It wasn't the same...and neither were we. We were no longer short, little people that had to tilt a head back to see the top of the ten foot tree...which was now adorned with a lighted, fancy, modern angel.

We were aware that things were changing. Christmas felt different. It was still joyful, always with great expectations but it wasn't just the ornaments and lights that were different. Things slip up on you and sometimes you don't notice.

Mom and Dad moved a bit slower. Their inner-light didn't shine as bright as it used to on Christmas mornings. It's the sort of changes you try desperately to ignore. But, like the fragile glass Christmas balls that hit the floor, there comes a time that you give in to the idea all is not what it used to be. Those two wonderful, vibrant people that gave their all to make sure we had an unforgettable Christmas, had begun to fade. And when you aren't looking and least expect it, they leave us.

Tradition is important. Savoring the moment is important. Hiding from the fact that things change doesn't alter that things will change and usually in ways that will change you too.

We've kept those honored traditions that Mom and Dad gave us. It was vital to them and as vital to us. It would be simpler to give in to the fast moving world that rushes through Christmas, only to rush through New Years and then speed through the next year. Repeat. That formula leaves us hollow and unsatisfied. We know deep within us that tradition keeps us together, bound by the past and yet living in the present and ignoring the future. Slowing down to watch a child rip into a brightly wrapped present is something to be cherished.

Christmas morning, my siblings and I rushed in to see what Santa brought. Caught up in the wonderful moments of dreams coming true. Then we would settle in, the eight of us and one present at a time was opened and ahhh-ed and oood-ed by all. Then the next present was opened.

We started at five in the morning and were still opening gifts at noon. It never got boring or tiresome because whatever was underneath that flashy wrapping paper held everyone's attention and was someone's dream being unwrapped. Watching the face register surprise would fill the room with laughter. We were taught to savor the moments. We knew that the next present could be ours. What mattered was dreams were coming true and we were all a part of it. Mom would say, "Be still and watch. Life is happening." It's a thought that could be applied year round.

"Be still and watch. Life is happening."

SALMON CROQUETTES

1 small can salmon with oil liquids
(Buy boneless/skinless, packed in <u>oil</u>.)
1/2 c. self-rising flour
½ c. corn meal
½ small onion
1 egg

Mix all ingredients.

Be sure to add the oil packing in salmon can.
Heat frying pan with two tbsps. of oil.
Spoon batter into a hot frying pan and fry.

Christmas and Good Cheer

All of the shopping, wrapping, anticipation and excitement come down to a bell ringing at five in the morning and little feet thumping towards the Christmas tree, while rubbing eyes and fighting off that time when one is half asleep and struggling to wake.

That's when the blurred eyes pop! Rocking Horse, tricycle, bicycle and for me a train set. All the grand unwrapped stuff Santa has left. We truly had been good and Santa noticed.

Dad, as far back as memory can unfold, has always announced Santa's arrival with a crystal bell. He would run throughout our home, clanging his bell, bedroom to bedroom, and shouting, "Get up! Santa has come!" His bell ringing-town crier would draw everyone from their beds and to the Christmas tree. The excitement was electric!

We would find our place on the floor and prepare for hours of unwrapping gifts. Mom had already started the coffee, so if someone was missing for a few seconds, you can bet they were pouring a cup of motivation and grabbing a sausage and biscuit, always on the stove top and waiting.

And so began the marathon of boxed dreams, unwrapped. One present at a time, we opened new shirts, underwear, cap guns and cowboy hats. Joy and laughter mixed with anticipation and excitement filled our home.

After all of the guessing, shaking and feeling, we

finally get to see what's in those shiny, happy boxes. The guessing was often wrong.

Mom and Dad in their playful way would box and wrap gifts in disguise. If you thought because the box was a shoe box that you were getting a new pair of sneakers...you are just as likely to be wrong. A set of Roy Roger cap guns fits nicely in a shoe box and therefore throws you off the path of guessing what's in the box. It's a gifting trick that we all learned and have often used, over and over.

Mom would slow the festivities by reminding us we had stockings to investigate. That usually signaled a break for the adults. Sausage and biscuit, a cup of coffee and stretching legs. Stockings hung on the mantle were filled with fruits, nuts and personal items like nail clippers, a comb or brush, matchbox cars, candy canes and chocolate marshmallow Santa's. Plenty to keep us busy while the adults refreshed.

Then back to opening the wrapped presents, one at a time. The smallest kids were always the elf's that helped Mom hand out the presents that were waist high around the tree. Trash bags were passed around and as each gift was opened the paper and ribbons filled the bags.

As the number of presents narrowed down and only a few left to open, for me was the saddest part of Christmas morning. It signaled the end and as much fun and excitement as we were having, I didn't want it to end.
But end it did and the boys would line the curb with filled bags of sheer joy now crumpled and ready for

disposal. The tree looked bare. The area under the tree so packed and filled with boxes only a few hours ago, is now empty. It all seemed a bit sad...until you remember the new cap guns and cowboy hat. Required items to re-live all the Paramount westerns and TV cowboy shows.

The kids would take their new toys and clothes to their room and would soon be on the driveway trying out the new remote car or Styrofoam airplane that you launch with a large rubber band.

Long before you are ready to give up the toys and settle in for Christmas Dinner, you are called in to sit at a feast of turkey, ham, handmade dressing, potato salad, brown and serve rolls, cornbread and a few Lebanese dishes...followed by an endless buffet of cakes and pies, all hot from the oven. No one could bake like Mom. Mississippi Mud pie-cake, white coconut cake, cherry pie, pecan pie, Italian Cream Cheese, dump cake, and a peach cobbler. My stomach stretches just remembering all of the amazing food and desserts. The required nap after such a lavish and endless meal gave time to settle down and reflect on what gifts you had gotten and given...and just how lucky a person can be.

All of the Christmas traditions that Mom and Dad established for our family, remain intact, today. I wake our grown kids and their kids with the ringing of the crystal bell, announcing Santa has come. We open one gift at a time, to savor the moments of both giving and receiving. Then the almost too much Christmas Dinner, nap that settles one down to reflect on how grand life is.

My siblings do the same. They live and re-live the bell ringing and town crier in all of their homes, too. We've added a few traditions that our kids enjoy and have begun passing those traditions to their kids.

When our daughter and her family were deployed in Japan, I would call her, ring the bell into the phone and shout out that "Santa has come, Get up!" for her two kids. We did that for six years, putting the phone up to sleeping grand kids. They are finally home safe, having retired from active duty. Now, along with her brothers and their families, all convene in our home Christmas Eve and prepare for an exciting Christmas. Beginning at five in the morning with the crystal bell ringing out, sausage and biscuits on the stove top and a feast-in-the-waiting, our kids and grandkids unwrap their dreams come true; one at a time.

Merry Christmas to everyone! Have a safe and healthy Christmas.

FRIED CHICKEN

1 whole chicken, cut up
1 cup buttermilk
1cup flour
½ tsp. salt
1½ cup. Wesson oil

In a large mouthed bowl, pour 1 cup buttermilk and add a dash of salt.

In a plate start with ½ cup of flour to roll chicken in. (add a dash of salt to the flour.)

On medium heat, heat oil for frying.

Dip one chicken piece in buttermilk, then roll in flour and place in hot oil.

Cook about ten minutes, turn to low and cover and cook another five minutes.

Turn chicken and cook another five minutes.

Using buttermilk, expect chicken to be crispy. Use whole milk if you prefer less crispy.

Roy Rogers Wears a White Hat

Mom and Dad would go to Otasco after the Christmas parade and pick out what they thought would make their six kids happy, Christmas morning. What we didn't know until we were adults is that Dad would charge everything and spend the next eleven months paying monthly Otasco payments to have last year's Christmas paid for in November...starting all over again the second week in December.

It was an endless trap that taught us to plan ahead, and not charge anything for Christmas. Dad did the best he could with eight people to care for. Money was scarce and with eight people, even more scarce. But the lesson wasn't lost. He was the genesis that all six siblings never vary from. Pay cash for Christmas.

He would "herd" us down to Washington Avenue, for the festive Christmas parade. The street power lines were covered in festive lights, reindeer and Santa's on every light pole and garland stretched up high, ran across the street. The bright lights and Christmas decorations were especially joyous after dark and all lit up. High school bands, an endless stream of themed floats, the Shriners in their funny looking hats rode tiny scooters. There were antique cars, fire engines, convertibles with stunning beauties waving their gloved hands. At the end of the parade was Santa in his sleigh tossing out handful after handful of candy. Kids scrambled leaving no candy unclaimed.

When the parade ended, Mom and Dad would walk us to the Paramount, buy our tickets and my oldest brother was given money to buy us popcorn and drinks. Now I'm not an avid pickle fan, but for whatever mystical reason I couldn't resist the whole dill pickles in a white sleeve bag. That pickle would last through a double feature. The smell of hot cashews made my mouth water. Back then hot cashews were a rare treat. They are even more rare today.

Free of kids, Mom and Dad would make their annual pilgrimage to Otasco's, to do their shopping...which always included a set of six shooter cap guns, for the youngest. I relished in being the youngest.

Maybe what brought that memory of the cap guns to the foreground is the present day news when a six year old child was suspended from school because he used his index finger as an imaginary gun. Mr. Freud, take a letter.

My generation grew up watching Roy Rogers and Trigger defeat the bad guys. We wanted to be like him, wear the white hat and chase after the bad guy in the black hat. Too many people wearing gray hats now and making the white hat, less white and the black less black.

I'm not surprised people are confused. We had it simple. Cheer on the guy in the white hat and boo the guy in the black hat. We played with cap guns and didn't dream that some idiot would come to school with a real gun. We were raised better. Therein lies the crux of the problem.

We can fold our hands and say the world has changed. Yes and no. There are silly things happening like the kindergarten kid that was suspended for his imaginary index finger gun. Actually it isn't silly, it's plain dumb. I bet if that kid were questioned by a responsible adult, he would know who wears a black hat and who wears a white hat. I bet he could tell you that his finger wasn't a death-weapon. I also bet because of the stupid and tilted way life is viewed today, he will never own a pair of Roy Rogers's cap guns. That's the sad part. He's being stifled and discouraged to have an imagination.

Imagination is what brings innovations, new products, a better life...and now it's being suppressed because people have grown lazy, stupid and over protective. Kids need to be pushed out in the yard to play physical games and get off the internet or video games. They need to know if a skunk sprays you, that you are going to stink for some time. Life is lived at Christmas parades and going to the movie theater is a treat, not an obligation. And most of all they need to know video games are not real life. They are an escape from real life.

The answer is simple; buy your kids and grandkids some trusty Roy Rogers cap guns. Let them breathe and enjoy chasing after the imaginary guy in the black hat. It's what heroes are made of. We can all be heroes by standing up to the bullies in the black hats that want to take away Christmas, our faith and our guns, and our children's imagination.

No one will ever experience the Christmases we've had or the childhood we enjoyed. That time has gone in many ways, but...we can hold on to our traditions and pass them on. Traditions are comfort, stable, no gray areas...it's white hat against black hat and as long as we cling to those principles and traditions and teach them to the youngest generation, they will be better equipped to stand up to a handful of bullies that think our world should be like they want it, which excludes Christmas, religion and the right to own cap guns.

Thank you, Roy Rogers for showing a generation that if you wear a black hat, expect the good guys to show up in their white hat.

HOMEMADE VEGETABLE SOUP

(Made ahead of time and frozen.)
1 gallon of tomatoes, chopped
2 quarts butter bean
1-quart whole kernel corn
1 head of cabbage, chopped
1 quart okra, chopped.

Cook butterbeans in 2 cups of water for 30 minutes.
Add everything else.

Cook until hot.

Let cool and freeze in 8-quart freezer bags.
You can add potatoes and meat when you thaw for
meal, or eat as is.

Fish Bait and Wisdom

Back in the day of the Mississippi Blue Law and when all of Greenville's merchants rolled up their carpets at eight pm every night and closed on Sundays, my brother and I got up before the fishes, stopped at Doc's Bait Shop for the Fisherman's breakfast special of a coke, a honey bun and live bait.

My brother, the eternal bargain shopper, picked up a Styrofoam minnow bucket and said, "Hey Doc. There's no price on your minnow bucket." Doc, not looking, bellows back, "five dollars." My brother, bellows back "But, Doc, I can get that same bucket anywhere in town for two dollars.

Doc, "Not at four in the morning, you can't."

One of many colorful characters of yesteryear. Doc of Doc's Bait shop in Greenville; dispensing wisdom, bait, and the best sliced baloney on this side of the levee.

Timing is everything.

PINEAPPLE UPSIDE DOWN CAKE

1 pkg. Duncan Hines butter recipe golden cake mix
½ c. butter (1 stick)
1c. brown sugar
1 can (1-lb. 4 oz.) whole sliced pineapples
Maraschino cherry, halved.

Preheat oven to 375*.
Melt butter in 13x9-inch pan.
Sprinkle brown sugar evenly in pan.

Drain fruit.

Set pineapple slices on top of brown sugar with
cherry halves in center of pineapple slices.
Mix cake as directed.

Pour batter over fruit.
Bake 40 minutes to toothpick test.
Let stand 5 minutes.

Turn upside down onto a large platter.
Serve warm.

Refrigerate, if there is any left over.

Naff Farris

Naff Farris, ran a small corner grocery store on Theobold Street. My Grandmother had a home right next door to Naff's. He was short, dark features and always talking nonsense. A gentle, kind soul that obviously loved people and could come up with some of the most off the wall sayings. Naff is a character that you soon do not forget. No man could have been any more loving or colorful.

"You give me a headache in my shoes." What does that mean?

My Mom and I went in Naff's for whatever it was she needed and down low where any five year old kid would be tempted, he kept an array of candies.

Being a kid, perhaps a naive kid, I pocketed a few of those candies. Later in the day, I was enjoying a piece of the candy when my Mom asked where I got it.

"Naff's."

She snatched my hand and pulled me all the way to the store. I was confused and had no idea what was happening. When we got to the store, Naff, in his usual manner had some nonsense thing to say when my Mom cut him off and told me to tell Naff what I did. I wasn't sure, but it must have been bad because my mom seldom got upset and she was way beyond upset with me.
"Show him the candy!"

I pulled out what I had left, still not sure what was happening.

"You stole that candy! Naff didn't give it to you...you didn't pay for it, did you?"

A shoulder shrug didn't work, although I tried a few of them, one after another.

"You give back what you stole from Naff. We don't steal! Tell him you are sorry and that you will never take something that isn't yours again."

I did as I was instructed and Mom paid for the candies that I had eaten. I put back what I hadn't eaten. I sure didn't want to. That was some good candy.

After we left the store, Mom sat me down and explained to me that taking something without paying for it was stealing and how bad stealing is.

Heck, the candy was right there at my line of sight, so I helped myself. I had no concept of money, buying or what stealing was until she calmly and lovingly explained what I did and how wrong it was.

I tell this story about myself for a reason. I was caught stealing, although I didn't know I was stealing. I was fortunate to have someone in my life that cared enough about me to explain the difference.
Take a stroll in Walmart. How many young mothers do you see that take the time to explain to their kid's proper behavior? I can't help but wonder how much

crime could be avoided if those tiny little people had someone snatch them up and make them go back to where they took something that wasn't theirs and made to apologize for their wrong doing.

Maybe I was a bit slow grasping what was happening to me at the time, but someone I respected, loved and trusted told me I did wrong.

Babies having babies. Maybe somewhere along their crooked road someone should have, or at least could have told them what the consequences are.

When Carol and I were at Delta Medical Center having our first child, we were twenty-one and excited about the birth of our first. I was standing at the glass enclosure staring at a tiny, new person that was soon going home with us. She was an amazingly beautiful newborn. Some of them were all red and wrinkly and cried a lot. Not our daughter! She had smooth skin, two inch long black hair and was laughing. She was a live doll. Tiny, but beautiful. Tiny is what scares most new dads. I was no exception.

While standing there an older woman, you know the type, prison matron-like was talking with a woman not much older than I. It took a moment for me to realize that she was the grandmother! Her daughter, thirteen years old had given birth and the matron was telling the new grandmother not to worry about the hospital bill...all of that was paid for by the Government. Our new born didn't come prepaid. We had to work and save for our new bundle of happiness. Then it occurred to me it takes nine months and the new mother was thirteen. The math is sad. What was even sadder was the new grandmother was asking what else the new mother could get from the Government. I had to leave. My blood has a flash point and I could feel it building. The last thing I wanted was anger at such a wonderful, happy time in our lives.

I left the glass enclosure and headed back for Carol's room. I remember thinking that someone, maybe the woman standing next to me wanting all of the Government programs she could get, should have taken her daughter back to Naff's Grocery Store and explained to her the difference between right and wrong. Say what you will, a thirteen year old girl, a child, hasn't had a childhood of her own and has now brought a new baby into this world. Someone should have been marched back to Naff's!

The whole scene of matron and new grandmother...."gave me **a headache in my shoes.**"

Pork Chops and Noodles

4 pork chops de-boned and chopped up
1 pkg. egg noodles
1 medium onion chopped
2 small cans tomato sauce
2 chopped cloves garlic

Brown pork chops.
Add onion and sauté, and then add tomato sauce, 2 cans tap water and garlic.

Cook noodles separate and add to pork chops.
Simmer ten minutes.

Add salt/pepper to taste.

An Injustice in School Sports

Parents know it, although seldom talk about it, but there's injustice in school sports. When you transition from Lourdes elementary to St. Joe, organized sports kicks in.

Our first born decided she wanted to play school softball. She was twelve. She had no past experience, only the desire to play. Here's what's amazing, she was twelve years old and in comparison to the St. Joe softball team, she was starting out twelve years behind.

Girls on the team had been playing since they were five, now they are seniors and have been playing ball for twelve years...and that's who she had to compete with to get on the field during a game. The coach had to win games to keep her job, so like most coaches she had to play her best players to increase the odds of her keeping her job.

One can understand that system, as much as it sucks, it's simply the way it is. So, your kid, the one without experience, ends up working hard in practice every day but never gets the opportunity to actually play in a school game.

There's too much at stake for the coach. There's no justice in the system. And, there's very little to keep a player that hasn't the experience interested...which means that kid loses all confidence, gets frustrated to the closed door policy and the next thing I knew she wanted to quit. The last thing you want to see is your kid quitting...anything, especially a sport she has learned to love and seems to have a natural knack for.

Ward Recreational Center offers summer ball. That is supposed to be a place where every kid gets to play, no matter their skill level. If that were only true.

Here's what happens in real life. Coaches that have been around for a while scout out the better players in past seasons to build a strong team. The day comes that a gaggle of kids gather and the coach's hand pick their team. The silent elephant in the room is, the inexperienced and to some degree the less talented are left standing, not chosen and without a team.

That's how our team was formed. Not to put a fine point on it, but the non-chosen, the less experienced was grouped together to form our team. For a clear picture, you have five teams made up of the better players and one team made up from the...inexperienced. The injustice just seems to snowball.

First day of summer practice, I am the only parent in the bleachers. Some roughneck that thought he could teach twelve year old girls something about softball, knew one language that was a bit raw for twelve year old girls. The first time he let loose a few foul words, I thought to myself, he's frustrated but certainly inappropriate.

The second time a string of four letter words came out of his mouth, I came off the bleachers and we had a one on one in private. He stomped off the field, never to return.

There's a team of eager, young girls that want to learn softball, including my own daughter and their coach; the roughneck, has departed in a huff. Guess who picked up a bat and started hitting balls to the girls? There was no choice, no options and no coach.

That first summer softball season was miserable. We lost every game we played. We usually didn't lose by a close margin. When we lost, it was a trouncing of double digits to zip. But, from the first of the season to the end, those girls fought their way to gain peer respect, which there was very little of. They worked harder than any employees I've managed in the work world. It was their determination that kept me going.

Two hours before a scheduled practice my daughter and I would practice the basics, over and over. And when the team showed up we practiced two more hours...and after practice my daughter and I would push out another hour of practice.

As a parent, it's amazing to watch one of your children reach for their goal. The sacrifices, the determination and the do or die energy was amazing to be a part of. It was my honor to watch my daughter become a young adult.

School started and after all of the endless hours of practice and even the humiliation of game loss after another, she now had experience. She had a skill set and a hunger that most athletes dream of. Yet, she spent that whole next school ball season, on the bench. Practices were grueling but the coach has her responsibility to the school to win. A second season was spent collecting splinters.

When Ward's summer softball came around our daughter wasn't the only novice with a bit of experience under the belt. This novice didn't scout other teams and try to scalp their players, rather I sit back and took the players that were not chosen. If there was only one team with integrity, it was our team. Winning wasn't everything; playing, participating and having fun was our objective.

We turned the corner that second season at Ward's and began winning games. Our team players were being scouted and considered for the better teams, but however it worked out, we ended up with the same basic team we had before...and they had been practicing off-season, often times with me and my daughter. Rain, snow, hot sticky weather didn't matter those kids were driven...and I still believe today they were driven because they knew they were going to play. They had a score to settle.

Next season at St. Joe. My daughter had been scouted by every summer season coach. They all wanted her in summer ball. Surely with that experience, she would play school softball. Nope. She rode that third season of school ball collecting more bench splinters. She toughed it out, stayed positive and looked forward to summer softball at Ward's.

The third season at Ward's was truly phenomenal. My daughter could hold down first base better than any kid in the entire league. She could burn any opposing player while playing short stop. She had amazing skills playing second base and in a pinch could hurl fairly consistent on the pitcher's mound. So much practice, and in so many different positions, she became an all-round player, good at any position and the best at most.

She had developed a mean stick and could consistently be counted on for a triple. Her team mates would have to pad their glove to catch her thrown ball. Strength, agility and sheer determination drove her to be her best. The team worked equally hard and developed at an amazing pace.

The level and caliber of players developed on that team were amazing. They were quick, accurate and carried a big stick. I was proud of every one of them! The distance they traveled from that first no-win season to an astounding no-loss season. Our team did so well we qualified for Regionals, then State and onto the World Series in Tulsa. There was much to-do about how great a player my daughter had become. On a scale of one to ten she went from a one to fifteen. Yep, pretty proud papa, I was.

At the World Series we played nail-bitter after another, competing against the finest teams from all over America. Our girls would get behind and fight their way back to win, time and again. The game that sent us home was a sixteen inning, sudden death and in a blink of an eye we had a run scored against us that ended our bid to win the World Series. We placed 14th out of 76 teams.

But, we won something in the World Series there's no trophies for. Our team defied the odds. Our team came from literally nothing, absorbed peer jeering and ridicule...and yet we qualified for and played in the World Series. Those jokers and jeering peers along with scouting, scalping summer league coaches and the school coach were nowhere to be found. They weren't at the World Series, but our team was.

In their minds and in their world of fighting back, they won something a lot more important than a series of games. They won self-respect, self-confidence and the knowledge that you can be a part of something bigger than a ball game.

I watched a group of girls, that I call my own, with little to no confidence that no one else wanted on their team, grow, develop and become fine young adults with memories no one can ever take away from them. They played in the World Series!

No parent could have been any more proud than I was and of my daughter that fought her way to the World Series, starting out twelve years behind.

It's not where you start but where you end up.

THANKSGIVING MEDLEY

THE TURKEY

1 - 18 lb. turkey
2 garlic cloves
1 stalk celery
salt/pepper to taste

Stuff turkey with celery and garlic: rub outside of turkey with salt/pepper. Wrap in foil and cook at 350* for 4 hours.

GIBLET GRAVY

1 can chicken broth
2 eggs, boiled and finely chop
lightly salt/pepper
2 tbsp. cornstarch

Bring broth to a boil and add eggs. Mix ½ cup cold water with cornstarch and add to broth. Cook on medium heat until thickens.

DRESSING

3 lb. chicken, boiled, cold and deboned.
2 pans cornbread crumbled fine.
Broth from chicken
2 sleeves of crackers
1 chopped onion
5 stalks celery, chopped
1 tbsp. sage and salt & pepper to taste.

Put broth in pan: add celery, onion, salt, pepper and sage. Stir. Add cornbread and crackers. Stir again. Put chicken in the dressing mixture, stir and cook 400* for 30 minutes, uncovered.

CHRISTMAS HAM

20 lb. ham
1 canned Coca-Cola
40-60 whole cloves

Select bone in ham. Trim fat and skin off. Stick whole cloves deep into the ham (40-60) making a close knit "web".

Cradle in foil, place in roasting pan and pour whole coke over ham. Seal the foil over ham and cook 4 hours at 350* or until done. (Or 18 minutes per pound).

Note: leave a little ham on the bone when trimming leftovers. Save the bone for a pot of pinto beans. Bone can be frozen until you are ready to cook pot of pintos.

Boys Will Be Boys

Our two boys. What can I say? They were boys, and I mean all boy-boys. The youngest was spoiled to Mom and Dad's real Christmas tree. We all were. The year we moved away from Greenville and knew that we couldn't drive back to Greenville that year for our annual Christmas with my parents, we did the unthinkable. We bought a fake tree. Wait. I bought a fake Christmas tree. Point that finger at me, please.

Everyone seemed fairly peaceful with the idea of our first fake tree, except our youngest son. Carol caught him one afternoon staring at the tree, decorated, lights and ready for Santa.

"What's up buddy?"

"Nothing."

That ended that.

A few days later he went rummaging in the garage. You do know a garage isn't for parking cars. That's a fantasy perpetuated by Hollywood. it's designed specifically to be a close-by junk room. A catch-all. We had boxes and boxes of stuff we hadn't gone through since the move. Someday we will get to it. Someday we'll use the garage for parking our cars like those people in Hollywood...just not today. Apparently we didn't need any of that stuff and had plenty of stuff already unpacked.

He found the box he was after and slipped away.

There's no telling what he's up to. They do that, them boys. They ponder on something for a while then put their plan into action.

About the time I pulled in the driveway coming home from work, remember I can't park in the garage like normal folks...I stopped short and was shocked at the sight. This seven year old kid had dug out his older brother's scout gear, found what he was after, a hatchet and walked down the neighborhood. You gotta see this coming. He did!... He "found" a live Christmas tree and cut it down. He was holding the hatchet in one floppy hand, dragging a tree taller than he was with the other hand. He was leaned into his labor like an old work mule.

We were new to the neighborhood and I remember thinking, I hope he didn't do what I think he did. Yep. Right out of a neighbor's front yard. What a grumpy neighbor. That guy was on fire. I calmed him down and explained that our youngest son was used to a real tree and this year we ...that is I, bought a fake tree. The guy wasn't having it. That was the most expensive Christmas tree I've ever bought.

Now picture the most scraggly, skinny tree, with only a few limbs. It was by far the ugliest tree I'd ever seen. What the neighbor was so hot to trot about escapes me. I wouldn't have wanted that in my front yard and would have paid someone to cut it down. But it was a real tree and since I paid a small fortune to calm the guy down; we took down the fake tree and decorated our most expensive real, live Christmas tree, ever.
Buyer's remorse wasn't part of the equation. We

never did befriend that neighbor. Our youngest son was forbidden to enter his yard...ever. Old Scrooge.

That was the beginning of our new home, new neighborhood, new job and new city, Chattanooga. If we had been in Greenville that Christmas, we would have made our annual visit to the St. Joe football field for a tree. I dropped the ball. I went fake.

About a year later our older son, now fifteen, had joined a climber's club and a spelunking club. We were not exactly thrilled with either choice, but we encourage our kids to expand, discover and grow.

I had a brand new camcorder. In that dinosaur era, progress had brought us to a shoulder mount, bulky home camera that Hollywood wouldn't use because of its over-size.

Oldest and youngest sons are in the garage, you remember the one filled with junk, boxes and everything but a car. What are they up to now? A friend came by and picked up both the boys. They were going on an adventure and promised to be home by dark.

On time, they arrived both beaming. Uh oh. You know deep down in your parent heart that they've been up to something you really don't want to know about.
The oldest, restless and excited hooked that bulky camcorder up to the TV. He hit play and said, "Watch this!" .....Uh oh!
He videoed our youngest son, now eight years old repelling off of a water tower. Talk about a sinking

stomach! He had taught our youngest son how to repel, that is slide down a rope from the top of a water tower! I wasn't sure if I should beat him then or wait to see the rest of the video to determine how severe that child needed a beating.

I watched the rest of the video...and the youngest filmed the oldest, Tarzan style repel from the water tower. My stomach churned. Carol kept both hands over her mouth, the entire video. I can't remember ever seeing her eyes bug out like that. We were stunned...they were proud of their accomplishment. We saw danger, they saw adventure.

We decided they needed grounding and an explanation that eight years old is way too young to be repelling a water tower. I hated to spoil their sense of accomplishment, but parents have to draw lines and this time a line had to be drawn. And by the way, you are not to take your little brother crawling around in caves. He's too young. Spelunking is for older kids that can scream loud.

Yep. That's my boys. One afternoon they pulled the trampoline over some distance underneath a tall, mature pine tree. Carol and I sat on the porch and watched them.

Carol "What are they up to now?"

Me "Guess we're about to find out."

The oldest watched the youngest bounce as high as he could, then stepped out into the trampoline and bounced him higher...high enough that the kid locked

arms around a limb twenty feet up.
"Oh my God!"

"Yes dear. That's our boys."

He hung there a few minutes, dropped into the trampoline giggling his young self, silly.

Not to be out done, the oldest son bounced and bounced harder until, yep, he latched on that limb, hung for a few seconds and let go. It's the letting go part that will take your stomach.

Their older sister, now pretty dang excited about trying it, jumped up on that trampoline and off she goes, up into the wild blue yonder until she gets high enough to lock on to the limb.

That's when Carol stood, looked away from our daughter dangling from a tree limb twenty feet up and said, "I've had enough. I'm going in. Holler if I need to dial 911."

Growing up kids. What an adventure!

It's the letting go...

MOM'S EGG IN A HOLE

With a small juice glass cut a hole in the center of a slice of white bread.

Butter a fry pan and drop bread into skillet.

Break open an egg inside the hole of the bread.

Toast and flip to egg white's done-ness.

Fry the hole, in butter for a small round toast.

A Charmed Childhood

Sometimes when I wear my Grandpa hat I worry
about the grandkids. Seems to me our way of life has
shifted and maybe that's not so good. Video games
and certainly a different world of cartoons bombard
those small tikes...and I wonder what it may be doing
to them.

Back in the day I could sit through a Ma and Pa
Kettle movie six times without getting up. Now there
are monsters, gore type killers, zombies that are way
too real for a kid to recognize the reality and play
acting. It all must be so confusing to them.

Where was the harm in watching the Three Stooges?
Their humor was over-stated and a kid knew the
difference. Wylie Coyote, there's a study in over-
drama...and always played well. Good wins, evil
doesn't.

Where are today's heroes? Who are they? If there
was a Miley, whatever her name is, that bounced
around on stage near naked and all suggestive back
in our day, the child would have been quietly sent off
to Whitfield.

Hollywood marriages that last about as long as a
rubber pair of flip flops. Back in the day we were not
so nosy about Hollywood and its inhabitants. We
didn't know or care what their political thoughts were.
Truthfully, I still don't. But they make their noise,
usually I think to garner news coverage.
We played outdoors until the street lights came on,

then scurried home. That was our curfew. More than often, Dad would open the back door and holler out our names. We came running. No questions asked. That holler overrode the street lights, every time.

We took meals at a specific time, everyday and we all ate the same thing. We sat at the same table, said the blessing and there was no TV, no video games and no cell phones. It was family and food and a time to discuss whatever was happening in our lives. Most of the best parental advice I got as a kid was at the dinner table, usually listening to what older siblings had to say and my parent's reaction. They were older and tested the waters before I did.

We knew the policemen, by name. Back then they were part of the community. They coached summer baseball and helped out at the YMCA. We felt safe, knowing they were always nearby.

We knew the firemen, a great bunch of guys that kids of our time looked up to.

We had school teachers that were involved in our lives. They had genuine interest and a direct connection to us. Some teachers affected our lives and the direction we traveled. They certainly helped to mold who we are. I can name a lot of teachers that I am still grateful to, five decades later.
Ours was a charmed childhood. It takes a village to raise a kid and our village of Greenville took that motto steps further. I can remember thinking as a kid if I was somewhere I wasn't supposed to be and ran into a neighbor, I was worried that neighbor would "turn me in" to my parents.

We had discipline in school but that was minor compared to what happened when we got home. Misbehaving simply wasn't tolerated.

Yep. It's safe to say the world has changed and I do worry about how the small ones of today will be affected. But then as a grandpa, I have the opportunity to tell them how it was…

…long ago in a faraway place where everyone lived a charmed childhood.

MOM'S HOMEMADE DONUTS

Here's a real treat.

Mom would lay out the canned biscuits, cut a center hole.

Heat a pan of 2 inch deep cooking oil to very hot.

Drop in the raw biscuits and fry to golden brown. (Cooks fast)

Dust with white powdered sugar.

Fry the "holes" the same way and dust with powdered sugar.

An International New Year

Living in Greenville, I can look back and recall just how spoiled we were. It didn't feel that way. If we wanted a pot of pintos, we ran down to Bing's or Kroger's and bought a bag of beans and a ham hock. Or if it were, New Year's Eve, we would buy a bag of black eyed peas, bacon for flavoring and a head of cabbage, all for the traditional good luck into the coming New Year.

When we moved to Chattanooga, we could find the Southern basics fairly easy and could lay in the traditional provisions assuring a new year filled with good luck and fortune.

When you are really far away from Greenville, like out of the country; finding pintos, black eyed peas and cabbage is not so easy. There's no big Kroger display with all of the New Year's traditional foods. There's no Bing's to run down the street to.

When Carol and I flew back to Greenville from Bermuda, part of our visit was buying a new suitcase and filling it with foods we couldn't buy in Bermuda.

When you enter a country, there's that country's Customs and Immigrations to go through, staffed by that country's employees. What they know and live is what their country offers...and in this case that wasn't pintos, or dried black eyed peas.

As we passed through Immigrations, and believe me you are treated the same on every arrival, known to the Immigration agents or not, they always scrutinized everyone that landed in Bermuda. That meant passport had to be in order and a copy of a work permit, allowing one to work in their country. Their inspections of all documents never varied. After you pass their Immigrations, you are sent to the next counter, which is Bermuda Customs. It's their job to assure you are not carrying contraband; that is anything illegal into their country. They don't play. It's serious business, completed by some very serious people.

As we moved into the Customs area and our suitcases were laid out on a counter, their questioning began. Do you have... Yada Yada...?

When the agent went to pick up that one suitcase filled with our traditional foods, it felt way too heavy for him, so he insisted on opening the one suitcase filled with food that we couldn't buy in Bermuda.

As he unzipped the large, heavy suitcase, the busted bag of pinto beans spilled out all over the table and floor. They were like Mexican jumping beans bouncing and scattering everywhere. Twenty pounds of pintos is fine contained in a bag, but when twenty pounds of pintos is unleashed and spread all over the Customs floor, the agent was pissed. He picked up a few beans and called his supervisor over. They were convinced we were carrying drugs or something illegal.

To listen to their conversation trying to determine exactly what we had was almost hilarious, but considering the circumstances, funny wasn't on the agenda. "These are too hard to eat. He says they eat them" Supervisor, "You can't eat them. Rocks are softer than these things. Pull them off to one side and search everything they have. Something is not right, here."

The Director of Customs, a fine Bermudian and friend came over to see what the commotion was. He and his wife had been over to our home and had some fine Southern cooking, Carol style...which means it doesn't get any better. But, he wasn't amused, nor was he friendly. He was strictly business, giving me that serious, doubtful look. "Get this mess swept up." he barked at one of the agents.

When I tried to explain that pintos is a Southern delicacy, no one was buying my story. It was obvious we were running contraband. Couriers of evil. They had honestly never seen dried pintos! They had never eaten cooked pintos!
We spent the next two hours wondering if we were going to be arrested. No joke. Customs and Immigrations in other countries is no joking matter. We were finally released.

The ordeal made me appreciate just how good we had it in Greenville. The freedom to buy dried beans and a fresh head of cabbage, black eyed peas, corn meal and all of the traditional New Year's foods. You really don't miss your water until your well runs dry. It's easy to be spoiled. We usually don't give another thought to picking up dried beans or a bag of corn meal...but this year, when you celebrate the New Year with your favorite foods, remember those very foods are contraband in other countries. The

Bermudians had never had a bowl of pintos, or fresh cooked black eyed peas and until Carol arrived, they never had cornbread cooked to Southern perfection. Makes me love our State and country, that much more!

Eat all the Southern delectables for fame, fortune and with the best of luck in the arrival of the New Year.

Happy New Year!

MEASUREMENTS

Liquid Measures

8 fluid ounces - 1 cup
½ pint - 1 cup
1 pint - 2 cups
1 quart - 4 cups
2 pints - 1 quart
1 pint - 16 ounces
1 quart - 32 ounces.

Other Measurements

1 pound of butter - 2 cups
1 pound of flour - 4 cups
1 pound of sugar - 2 cups
1 pound of rice - 2 cups
1 pound of cracked wheat - 3 cups
1 pound lentils - 2 1/3 cups
1 pound pecans in shell - cups shelled

Peasant Blouse

1957, I was nine, almost ten years old. A couple of friends and I went to the Paramount to see a cowboy movie. Of course all three of us had our cap guns strapped on, cowboy hats and ready for action. It was our duty to help the good guy beat out the bad guy. We knew if we put the caps in our guns, we would be tossed out, so we went without ammo.

What we didn't know was it was a double feature and the cowboy played second. We had to endure the first movie, which wasn't a cowboy. I wasn't sure what it was, but I knew my guns would stay holstered.

I recall my buddies were bored enough that they were throwing popcorn at each other and we were warned to be quiet and behave or we would have to leave the theater. That made very little difference for the two guys having their popcorn war.

Well into the movie is when it happened. One step away from childhood and a small step over to a very young manhood. It's a scene I can still visualize.

As the diver surfaced the water and began to lift into the small row boat, her peasant, low cut blouse and all the water beads running everywhere was a stunning sight. Even the guys stopped their popcorn fight and were awe-struck. I remember one of them, maybe Kirby said, "She ain't got no bra on!"

Sophia Loren, eased herself up on the side of the

boat and paused. There was a hush that went throughout the theater. Time froze. Hearts raced. Boys set boyhood aside for the moment. She was captivating, exciting and filled the scene with her presence.

The hushed moment ended all too quick when the camera moved off of Sophia and on to a very lucky Allan Ladd. The intensity vanished, but what was once a less than attentive audience became fans. I know I did and fell right into the storyline plot of, "Boy on a Dolphin."

Strange how moments stick with a guy, especially moments like that. Sophia Loren, immediately gained a life time fan.

I lost count how many times I watched the movie, over and over, for that one frozen, exciting moment. When the cowboy feature did come on, the plain Jane hero's girlfriend didn't hold a candle. There were no water scenes with Sophia emerging in her wet, low cut peasant blouse. Cowboy movies lost some of its flavor that day.

Fast forward a couple of years, sitting in Coach Ferguson's eighth grade math class at E.E. Bass. Two rows over, three seats back was a stunning brunette. I can't explain the chemistry. She wasn't surfacing the water, all wet but she held my attention even greater than Sophia.

We met a few weeks later, as soon as I could untie my tongue and stop the jitters. I don't remember exactly how it happened but she allowed me to carry her books class to class...often making me late for my next class. Whatever punishment the teacher had for being tardy, I didn't care.

It was months before we actually held hands, but when we did, it was natural. I think, no I remember exactly, three days before the end of the eighth grade, I got my first cheek kiss. I couldn't have been happier. The lip-lock was a long time away.

School years came and went and we had each other. Whatever the world was doing didn't seem to matter to us. Flower children, drugs, free love, psychedelic music, Jimmy Hendricks, Bay of Pigs all took a back seat. We would sit on a park bench and talk for hours about what we wanted to do with our future. I will admit Janice Joplin caught my attention, but for whatever else was going on, we were oblivious.
All either of us wanted was to get high school behind us and get on with our future.

Finally, we walked the aisle at St. Joe's Catholic Church, November 10, 1967. It was a simple ceremony performed by Father Massina and attended by family and friends. I left my cap guns at home.
...That was forty-six years ago.

I still enjoy a good Sophia Loren movie wet or not, but...

...**nothing compares to the girl two rows over and three seats back.**

EGG CUSTARD

1 tbsp. flour
3 eggs
1 c. sugar
1 ½ c, milk
½ stick margarine

Put 1½ cups milk and ½ stick margarine in saucepan.
Heat margarine liquid and milk is scalded.

Beat eggs, flour and sugar on low with blender.
Add to milk & butter mixture in saucepan.

Stir to mix.

Pour into unbaked pie shell and sprinkle with 1/3
nutmeg.
Bake at 300* for 20-30 minutes.

Watch edge of pie shell for done-ness.

Mother Nature Goes Bad

Mother Nature sings her familiar song in the Mississippi Delta and we rejoice in what we know, understand and expect from her.

And then there are times that she takes a running fit and throws the unexpected at us like a jilted lover left at the altar. It was one such summer in 1973, that her fury, her bizarre retaliation to whatever evil-doing we may have been doing to her and her animal kingdom that she had enough and decided it was time to teach us respect.

Bob came over one afternoon all excited. Now Bob has a streak of Cajun in him as wide as three wild and stubborn mules. When he gets excited you may hear a few French words you haven't heard before. We won't test to see if they were profane or mundane but my instincts tell me mundane and Cajuns are incompatible.

"It's happened! They are as big as lobsters. Joking, I'm not."

Not a clue what Bob was talking about I tried to calm him, so he could tell me what his excitement was all about. In time he simmered a bit and told me that mud bugs are his favorite food. He grew up catching and eating mud bugs as far back as he could remember.

Okay, I got it. He's telling me crawfish are in season

and he has a hankering.

Actually it went a lot deeper than that. Mother Nature had for some bizarre reason pushed backwater into cotton fields and soybean field, all over the Mississippi Delta. Within that back water flush came a breed of crawfish never seen before. They were as large as lobsters, quadrupled their normal size and thousands of them, literally everywhere. Bob had trouble containing himself.

I need to stop here and tell you that Bob is a Giddy up buddy. Whatever hair brain ideas I came up with Bob was all in. He never questioned what the outcome would be, he simply said, "Giddy up." So when he came over all excited, a guy that never flinches, I had to go along with his one and only adventure.

Bob was determined to take advantage of the freaks of nature, Mother Nature's vengeance against us, and the only way to calm Bob down was to agree to go crawfish hunting. I was of course dubious. Crawfish are tiny and it takes fifty of them to make one good plate for a growing boy. The way Bob was talking, that same growing boy would be satisfied with a couple of these jumbo mud bugs. Impossible!

He insisted we stop at Walmart. He needed something to put the catch in. I agreed, since it was obvious Bob would not settle down until he completed his mission.

A friend of his told him about the freaks and where he had seen a billion of them. I'm more than a little skeptical and thinking maybe his friend had been busy with a mason jar full of clear liquid that had him seeing jumbo mud bugs and pink elephants.

I waited in the car and Bob, smiling like he had just won the lottery came out of Walmart with a fifty-five gallon plastic trash container.

"I hope this is big enough." He said as he got in the car. I think I rolled my eyes. If I didn't, I should have.

Twenty minutes later we were almost to Leland when Bob turned off the highway onto a dirt road and into a cotton field. We drove a few minutes and Bob slammed on the brakes. The dirt road was black and moving. I have never seen so many crawfish and the size of those bubbas was mind boggling, mason jar or not.

Bob, Bless him, couldn't wait to get his newly bought fifty-five gallon container out of the car and into use. I hate to admit this but he actually scooped literally hundreds of massive size mud bugs into the container and within moments they were boiling at the top of the container. Monsters. They were so big it was staggering. The snap on lid kept them contained.

Thirty minutes later we were at my home on Ely Lane and Bob was trying to decide if he wanted to shrimp boil them or what. Carol had one look and walked away. She wanted nothing to do with them and frankly I was a bit leery myself. Not Bob, he charged ahead and put on the first batch to boil, licking his chops. The shrimp boil smelled tempting.
With the first batch boiled, potatoes, onions, corn on

the cob and all the Cajun stuff we could find in the kitchen went into the second batch. Over the evening I lost count of how many batches we cooked. Carol was nowhere to be found.

The more I looked at the oddities, the more I wondered if they had been contaminated with radioactive waste, you know like the horror movies we watched as kids with giant ants and behemoth sized honey bees. I decided Mother Nature was truly pissed.

Whatever we as humans had done must have been epic. Mud bugs the size of lobsters, ain't right. I began to back away as Bob set him a plate out and dove into the first batch, now cooled. He groaned and moaned like he was at a Japanese masseuse and had a hundred pound woman walking on his back. He couldn't wait for the other batches with potatoes, corn and onions...or Bob called them on-yons.

He encouraged me to have a plate and well, I couldn't get out of my mind the radioactive honey bees bigger than a cat. I declined.

Bob bagged up his now cooked catch and took them home to stuff into his freezer. I didn't keep any. Carol wouldn't enter the kitchen until the freaks of nature were gone. She told me later that the mud bugs gave her the willies.

All in all, Bob's dream had come true. He was as happy a guy as I've ever seen. I was happy for him; although I was a bit concerned that he may glow in the dark.

The oddity, the strange mud bugs never happened again...that I am aware of; crawfish being flushed by back water into fields, quadrupled their normal size. Whatever we did to piss off Mother Nature we must have learned the lesson and haven't been so stupid, since.

She has a temperament and we tested her. According to Bob, we won. According to history, man never wins over Mother Nature; not for long, anyway. We may fool ourselves into thinking we defeated her but she has her ways, she has her wrath.

The next time I see crawfish the size of lobsters...and by the thousands in back water slush, I'll know we've managed to piss her off again.

She may not be so nice next time.

MOM'S HOMEMADE JELLY

1 box sure gel
1 gallon plums

Place washed plums in large stock pot.
Boil plums until they pop open.
Pour plums into a large colander with small holes and spoon press all the juices out of the plums.
Discard pulp and seeds left inside colander.

Measure out sugar (see sure gel box) and set aside.
Heat extracted plum juice, add sugar.

When you add sure gel, be ready to pour into sterilized jars. The sure gel works fast. Sterilize jars and boil tops and rings. Have them nearby for quick filling when sure gel begins to thicken.

Pour jelly into jars, place hot seal to preserve.
Turn upside down to check seal is good.
Add ring top. Use tart plums, usually small ones. This recipe will make 5 pints.

Never double recipe. Make one batch at a time.

Note: See granny hill's homemade biscuits. They are a perfect match for her plum jelly.

The best plum jelly comes from the mid-sized tart plums. Therein lies the secret to the best plum jelly.

Resolute

New Year's Day, a day of Resolute.
To affirm, set your course of determination, to commit.

Did you know our U.S. President sits behind a desk named Resolute? Without getting into the politics; the desk and resolute as you and I know it, aren't the same thing.

Resolute was a British sailing ship that went in search of a missing British explorer in the Artic. Bogged down in ice, the ship was abandoned. America and Great Britain were at odds. Seriously at odds about a lot of political matters of the day. We're talking at odds enough to go to war over. An American vessel found the abandoned ship and gave it to the U.S. Government who re-fit it and sailed it to England as a gift to Queen Victoria, as a peace offering.

Not long after, the Resolute was dry docked and sent to be dismantled. Queen Victoria had two desks made from the timbers of the Resolute. She kept one and sent the other to the U.S. President in 1880, as a good will gesture and a move that placed Britain and the US back in good graces with each other.

So what we ended up with is a desk made from the timbers of a ship that failed its mission and was abandoned. So much for Resolute.

Too bad the desk named Resolute doesn't actually mean Resolute. Our Country could use a bit of the real thing about now.

It's an odd word to start the New Year with. A New Year is akin to a new sunrise. It's an opportunity to start new, a fresh beginning. We have three hundred and sixty four other days a year to start over. How is it that this one day is supposed to make the difference?

I suppose there's no answer to that question, other than we all want to be better than we are. Sometimes, and maybe most times that's a good thing. But, what if we are happy with ourselves? What if life is so good to us that we don't want change? Should we resolute to not resolute?

Growing up the Mississippi Delta, life was simple. I don't recall being unhappy about what I didn't have and those around me taught me to be happy with what I did have. Now that didn't stop me from wanting better, only remaining happy until I earned better. It's a Delta thing I believe, because as we traveled the world and was exposed to other thought processes and other cultures, I discovered the uniqueness of how Southerners, especially those from the Greenville area, appreciate.

We didn't have our new neighbors in other parts of the country show up at our doorstep with a cake or pie to welcome us to the new community. That's a Greenville thing. We were neighborly. I found in other places people stayed to themselves. They didn't have that 'never met a stranger' attitude that was prominent in Greenville.

I had to leave Greenville to discover and appreciate her many, many treasures. Hindsight is always one hundred percent.

Maybe we shouldn't start the year off with a word like Resolute. Maybe, just maybe we would be better off taking on the word APPRECIATE. It's the Greenville thing to do.

Rather than make a list of things we want different, it's a thought that we could, if we choose, make a list of the things we appreciate.

It's everyone's choice...

Resolute or Appreciate.

Happy New Year!

WALDORF SALAD

3 c. apples, cored and diced

1 tbsp. lemon juice

2 c. diced celery

½ c. raisins

¼ c. broken walnuts

1/3 c. mayonnaise

Mix, toss and refrigerate for one hour before serving.

The Wisdom of Truman

Every bow season my three brothers and I would spend a week at Delta Pineland. One year I decided to spend two months in preparation, getting my bow sited in and knowing what I would hit at whatever distance.

Otasco had a new re-curved bow made of some very light alloy. I've tried to remember the metal content but as you read on you'll understand why remembering the alloy name has become a very insignificant detail in my memory. The bow, as I said was incredibly light, easy to handle and was made so a lefty could turn the bow upside down and shoot it left handed. For you left handed hunters, you know you have two strikes against you before you step one foot in the woods...unless you have a thick wallet and can afford the specialty left handed bow.

I bought the bow two months before hunting season, picked up a bale of hay, lots of balloons and a paper target of a deer. Endless hours followed. The new bow was a dream and as any hunter knows there becomes a bond-like attachment to good equipment. It's kind of like wearing your lucky socks. Everybody has a lucky pair of socks.

As the big week closed in, I got better and better at thirty, then forty yards and deadly to some small balloons. The deer target was so full of holes I had to finally take it down. I can't begin to guess how many arrows vanished somewhere deep into the hay bale and thin air.

I packed up my VW, thinking and re-thinking what all I would need. I carefully stored my new bow in the back seat...and off to my week of hunting with my brothers. We had the same camp site every year on one farm that was located in the heart of Delta Pineland. I was the last of the four to arrive. My brothers had unloaded, set up camp and one brother had his campfire stew brewing.

As I unloaded my gear, my bow in the back seat had shifted and half of it was sticking out. A friend of one of my brothers came by and slammed the car door to pass by, breaking my new bow. All of that practice and all of that time invested in that great bow went up in smoke. I was as depressed as any hunter with buck fever. There I was in excellent company and in one of the best hunting areas in the Greater South and I literally had nothing to hunt with. Talk about a ruined hunt. Kicking a few rocks didn't help.

That's about the time Uncle Truman showed up. He's a master hunter and a great guy. The first thing he did was ask what my brother had in the campfire stew. I remember that amazing laugh of Uncle Truman's. It was contagious. Problem is, I wasn't ready to laugh. My mind was spinning towards how I was going to hunt the next morning when the season opened.

My attention went back to Uncle Truman. He chastised my brother for making a campfire stew with store bought meat. He grabbed up one of my brother's bow and quiver. "I'll be right back." He disappeared in the woods and was back in ten minutes with two long, plump jack rabbits.

Truman had the rabbits dressed and in the pot in a flash. He stepped back and told my brother; the cook, "Now you got a real campfire stew."

The first time I went dove hunting with Uncle Truman, I had six birds in my bird vest. From the way his bird vest looked, he didn't have any. I was hot and sweaty and exhausted from carrying around all the birds in my backpack. A dove cried out, spooked and went to flight. Truman dropped that bird almost at his feet. He took two fingers ripped out the breast and slid it in his bird vest, packed with a large number of bird breast.

Sometimes the simplest things can make me feel dumb. I'm carrying around all of the bird carcass and Truman saves only what he plans to eat, the breast. I never carried a dove carcass again. Lesson one.

Lesson two came when he called me and asked if I wanted to run trot lines with him, I jumped at the chance. Here's a lesson for you fisherman that take home catfish; nail their head to a board, cut around the neck line and skin a catfish with a pair of pliers. Not Truman.

He would check a line and when a fish is on, he would flip the fish onto the boat seat and with the sharpest fillet knife I've ever seen, he would zip the catfish steak on one side, flip the catfish over and fillet the other side and toss, I promise you, the catfish skeleton back in the water. My eyebrows almost slipped of the top of my forehead when I watched a skeleton swim away from the boat! Again he kept only what he planned to eat. I didn't know my uncle was Daniel Boone.

As a side note he was famous for growing tomatoes the size of cantaloupes. I know, almost too much to absorb. It's one thing to have a tomato sandwich with a slice of tomato that hangs off the side of the bread, but to have a tomato so big one slice would make three huge sandwiches is almost too much for any Southerner to believe.

The next morning I had resigned myself that I would have to drive back to town and buy another bow when one of my brothers loaned me an extra bow. Truman, one brother and I paired off to hunt a section we had scouted weeks before. The ground was churned and choppy, saplings were stripped.

The area was loaded with deer activity. Single file my brother took the lead, Uncle Truman was second and I was last in line, as we made our way through some thick underbrush.

Truman stopped dead cold. His arm went up to stop me from taking another step. His index finger went to his mouth. My brother turned to see why he stopped and Truman gave him the signal to freeze.

Slowly Uncle Truman pulled an arrow from his quiver, loaded it and without a sound and any movement detected he let loose his arrow. Just below the head a water moccasin was now nailed to a tree that my brother was about to go under. The snake was less than a foot from my brother's head. No doubt Uncle Truman saved his life by taking a chancy shot. I'm not sure given the same circumstances that I could have made a shot with my brother's head so close, much less nail that sucker to a tree.

Without a blink he sliced the snakes head off and stuffed the snake in his hunting jacket. That night was the first time I've ever eaten snake. Lesson three, always take the shot.

My brother and Uncle Truman both got a deer. I got a case of ugly talk, trying to shoot a bow that I'd never shot before. After the fourth deer, I quit counting how many I missed.

That afternoon I drove to Otasco and they didn't have another bow like the new one I had bought. I bought another bow but I knew you don't walk in the woods with a bow that you haven't practiced with and expect to get a deer. Although I did as Uncle Truman said, always take the shot.

While the hunt was ruined for me that year, I learned a lot from Uncle Truman and the time I had with him was a learning class of life, survival and all with a great sense of humor.

Always take the shot - Truman Hill.

The Concert

March, 1975 I get a phone call from my sister that lives in Jackson. She was as excited as I've ever known her to be.

Carol and I were eight years married and I thought her infatuation over a guy from the past that I didn't like was over. It wasn't. Maybe a bit dormant, but alive and well.

My sister told me she had gotten some really hard to get tickets for a concert. I wasn't too happy but Carol, well she was thrilled. The concert was a couple of months away, completely sold out, and how my sister fangled tickets, I never questioned. She was as nuts about this guy as Carol was. I didn't see the attraction. I was content, without him in our lives. No man married to any woman wants to know that she has a "thing" for another man. It was obvious, I was jealous.

The two girls, my sister and Carol, talked for hours on the phone trying to decide what to wear and how to wear their hair. You know that girl stuff that usually has the guys headed for the nearest bar.

The time grew closer and their phone conversations grew longer and more frequent. Geez.

The coming event disrupted our quiet daily lives in Greenville. We had two kids attending Lourdes Elementary and what with all the dark headed kids in the same school uniform, they all looked like brothers and sister and if you weren't careful you could easily take the wrong kids home. Carol was distracted thinking about the event, but somehow managed to bring home the right kids every day, although a few that weren't ours did make it as far as getting in the van.

I went along and that's what I was, a non-participative, tag-along. I think Carol called me a bore. Maybe it was something else. When we got to the coliseum and climbed enough steps to be just this side of Heaven, we sat in a massive flow of humans, excited, motivated and anxious for the show to begin. I yawned.

And then it happened....the Space song...and HE walked out on stage. The electricity was astounding. Not one stadium seat had a butt in it. Everyone was standing, cheering, whistling, and hollering. One of our own had come home and no one, not a single person has ever gotten a welcome home like he did that day.

He began singing but you couldn't hear much over the absolute roar of the masses. It was like some guy had a mega-microphone inside an active bee hive. Buzzing like I've never heard before. Slowly, gradually the roar was pulled down and most, certainly not all, took a seat. It was then, from the nose-bleed section that I got my first look at my wife's, "other man." I no longer felt threatened. I had never experienced mass hypnosis.

The guy had captured everyone in the coliseum, including me and he wasn't half through the first song. Whatever jealousy or whatever that was, dissipated. Only a stuffed-shirt fool would have sat through the next two hours of non-stop, totally engaging entertainment and not been moved. Not even a bore.

This was more than an event. It was a life-event and one that was happening all around me. He played the house as if it was his last concert.

It's actually hard to describe and something that one must be present to really appreciate. It was the only time Carol and I saw Elvis live in concert. He was amazing.

I was wrong to begrudge Carol.

Years later as Station Manager for Republic Airlines at Chattanooga, I did something that no other manager had done before. I invited eight travel agents to fly from Chattanooga to Memphis, to see our hub. Lunched at Mud Island and last stop was Graceland. Lord, I had women falling on his grave. I questioned my sales efforts and wondered what the devil I was doing there. The airline has a sales department and why am I trying to boost the Chattanooga passenger loads? After prying three of the women off the grave, we took the indoor tour of Graceland. There, in the long hallway museum is where I realized the charity work that Elvis did in his lifetime. Everything from Boy Scouts to St. Jude. It was truly a stunner to see what all this guy accomplished and the staggering amount of his wealth that he shared.

In that hallway, for the first time I read the plaque

from the State of Mississippi, thanking Elvis for the 1975 concert, of which he donated all income from that concert to the Governor of Mississippi, who in turn presented to the Mayor of McComb, Mississippi with the proceeds to help out the tornado victims in McComb and Southern Mississippi area. It was the concert that Carol and I attended in Jackson. I had no idea it was a charity event paid for by Elvis. He donated everything to the tornado victims and paid his own expenses.

Ten years after his death, I'm in his home with eight very emotional women and all I could think about was how generous he was.

I made that trip nine more times with eight new travel agents at a time. The sales effort worked. Our business went through the roof. The travel agents sold our Memphis hub like crazy. But I wanted to go back because every time I went, I learned more about how generous Elvis was.

I was so moved by him, the live concert and all trips to Graceland, that my first novel was about, guess who? Yep. Someday I'll dust that novel off, clean up all the errors and submit it for publishing.

Treat me like a fool.

KATTAWAR FAMILY HOT TAMALE RECIPE

While the recipe looks complicated, it isn't. It is however, time consuming. As a family, Carol and I invite our two sons and their spouses and our daughter and her husband over, spreading out the work load. Each brings their own empty pot. One recipe makes 8 dozen hot tamales. If you have any leftovers, they freeze well.

We've discovered that doubling the recipes isn't a good idea. We make one full recipe for each pot. Each couple takes home their pot with 8 dozen tamales home, ready to be cooked. Your cook pot should be at least 8-10 inches deep and at least an 8 quart, best if it's a 10 quart size.

Inside stuffing:

1 lb. ground pork
3 lbs ground chuck
2 oz. chili powder
1 tsp table salt

2 tsp garlic salt (we have since revised the recipe to use fresh garlic (2 medium sizes cloves, pounded into a paste. chip up garlic into a wooden bowl. sprinkle salt, about ¼ tsp over garlic and pound with a pestle until garlic is a paste.) note a pestle is a hand held wooden tool like a pharmacist uses to grind pills.

Outside mixture

8 cups of self-rising corn meal
4 beef bouillon cubes
3 tsp. chili powder
1 tsp. table salt
5 ½ cups hot water (you will want your hot water, really hot. it has to melt the Crisco.)
2 ½ cups Crisco shortening
2 garlic cloves pounded into paste.

Sauce

4 oz. chili powder
1 tsp. Table salt
2 garlic cloves pounded into a paste
4 beef bouillon cubes

Mix all of the sauce ingredients together and set aside.

Corn shucks

Boil shucks until tender. Set aside to cool. Most any Kroger sells corn shucks in the Latino aisle.

Cut kite string into 10-12 inch strands. You will need about 100. This function usually goes to our 12 year old grandson. He is our official string cutter.

Mix inside stuffing in a large bowl.

Mix outside stuffing in a separate large bowl.

Take one corn shuck (cooled), spread open and flat. With a tablespoon scoop a full spoon of corn meal mixture and place on shuck in middle. With the back of the spoon, spread mixture flat leaving the last inch of shuck at top empty. (This allows your tamale to expand while cooking without cooking out of the tops of the shucks.)

Then take a full table spoon of meat mixture and roll in palm of hands to look like a small hot dog and place center of the meal mixture on the shuck in the cornmeal mixture. Take the closest side of the shuck to you and fold over away from you. Turn tamale to make opposite side face you and take that side of shuck and roll away from you making a full roll up. (You are spreading the corn meal mixture to first one side of the meat mixture, then rolling the tamale from the other side, coating both sides of the meat with corn meal.

Once you have rolled the tamale your bottom of the shuck is tucked upwards towards the "seam". When you have three tamales rolled, place the three seams towards each other, double wrap a kite string around the tamale and tie into a knot. Do not pull string so tight it will force the tamale to push out at the top.

Place a three-roll, standing up in pot of sauce you set aside earlier. Continue placing three-rolls upright into the pot until you have filled your pot...which is usually the full recipe of 8 dozen tamales.

The final count may vary depending how much corn meal and meat mixture you use on each tamale. Don't be alarmed if your recipe comes out with six dozen. That only means you have fatter, bigger tamales. The reverse is true, as well.

Last step is to fill pot with water about two inches above the top of the tamales. If you are having a tamale "party" and have friends over. They will take their tamales home without the added water. Add water when you get your tamales home and are ready to cook them.

Start tamales on high on your stove top. When the water begins a soft boil, cover the tamales and lower heat to medium. Cook for 2-3 hours after 2 hours of cooking take a three pack out and test-taste. You can tell if they need to cook longer, but usually 2 ½ hours on medium is just right.

Some helpful hints:

If you have leftovers, allow tamales to cool and place one dozen per freezer bag with a cup or so of cooking sauce. You'll use the cooking sauce to re-heat the tamales, stove top.

Also, if you make homemade chili, the tamale cooking sauce is a perfect addition to add texture and flavor to your home made chili. Don't toss away any leftover tamale cooking sauce. Freeze it in a freezer bag.

Most large grocery chains carry ground pork in one pound packs. We never use ground beef, only ground chuck. Rather than buying the more expensive smaller tins of chili powder, we usually buy the large chef-size at Kroger's.

If you clean as you go, the process is more organized. If you have one team building the meat mixture and another team building the corn meal mixture, have them clean up their work area before everyone sits to roll.

We place the shucks, meat and corn meal mixture in the center of the table, community style and everyone takes what they need, as they need it.

What could be a labor intensive process becomes a family or friend gathering to visit and catch up on each other, and at the end, everyone leaves with eight dozen tamales.

Tamales in 2014 cost $12-14.00 a dozen when you buy them ready made.

If you make them at home your cost is about $3.00 a dozen, about 75% savings.

You choose your own fresh ingredients and can control the taste. The above recipe is mild and generally acceptable to young kids. You can kick up the spicy by adding black pepper to the cornmeal mixture and hot sauce to the meat mixture for a more adult-spicy hot tamale.

In our home we enjoy tamales with homemade chili poured over them. If we prefer them a little spicier, we add hot sauce to our individual serving of chili, and then pour spiced up chili over the hot tamales.

Enjoy!

KIBBEE

3/4 c. cracked wheat (#1 grade)
1/3 tsp. allspice
1 lb. ground round
½ tsp. ground cinnamon
¾ tsp. black pepper
1 tsp. salt
1 medium onion, grated
¼ tsp. cayenne pepper

Pour dry cracked wheat into empty bowl. Run very hot tap water 3 inches over cracked wheat. Stir wheat to break up dry pockets in bottom, rinse and drain. (This removes any impurities and as mom says, rinses out the trash). Refill with hot tap water to 3 inches over wheat, let soak 20-30 minutes.

Place one pound of lean ground round in medium size stainless steel mixing bowl. Add all spices, grated onions and let sit while cracked wheat is soaking.

Hand squeeze cracked wheat, removing water and add to meat mixture. Mix all ingredients by hand. Nayeh (raw kibbee) tastes better at room temperature.

Note: select round steak, have butcher trim fat and grind. Mom always used ground round for kibbee, taking her time selecting only the finest round steak to be ground. She never used pre-packaged ground round from the meat department. Select your own and have butcher remove the fat and grind.

Onions are grated by hand, not chopped in electric chopper. While kept a secret, mom always added a dash of cayenne pepper to her kibbee. If you make a larger meal than one pound, double ingredients by the number pounds of meat. After you have it mixed to nayeh, taste test and add spices to your liking although, the above spices are pretty close to the flavor you are expecting.

Cabbage Rolls

2 medium sized head of cabbage
3 lb. ground chuck
2 lb. ground pork
1 lb. long grain rice
1 large onion, chopped fine
1 tsp. salt
½ tsp. black pepper
¼ tsp. of cinnamon

Core a medium head of cabbage cutting deep in and around the core and remove the core. (Discard). Place cabbage head in a deep pot adding water over the top, cored out hole facing up. after about twenty minutes of boiling, with tongs you can begin pulling one leaf of cabbage at a time off of head and placing it on a nearby plate to cool.

In a separate large and deep pot, add one tbsp. of Wesson oil and chop up large pieces of one white onion. Cook on low for 5-8 minutes to lightly brown the onions. Set off to cool. (Flavoring the pot).

In a large mixing bowl combine all ingredients and mix by hand. With your large bowl of mixture in the center of the table, take one single cabbage leaf and place 3 heaping tbsp. of meat and rice mixture to the inside, bottom or core/vein end of the leaf and spread meat mixture out similar to a small hot dog. Then roll one revolution and tuck left and right ends inward and roll up. Place in pot seam down. Continue to roll until all meat mixture is used. Cover the bottom of the pot with the first layer and stack the second layer on top, etc.

Cover all layers with water, placing two or three small saucers on top the keep them from floating. Bring water to a boil. Boil 10 minutes reduce heat to simmer.

Cook 2 ½-3 hours.

Using large leaves and rolling large cabbage rolls runs the risk of the center of the cabbage rolls being dry. For best results buy medium head of green cabbage. Roll small.

Remember to squeeze fresh lemons and lightly salt over the cooked cabbage rolls for an incredible flavor.

About the Author

Ron Kattawar, the youngest of six, was born July 19, 1948. It was a magical time when the Mississippi Delta had become a gathering place of literati, and was in an amazing economic growth boom. Segregation was a part of everyday life. Kids lived a simple life.

Within his home, his father, Mike Kattawar Sr. was a factory worker at U.S. Gypsum Mill and a strong disciplinary. Dollie Kattawar, came from a large family of ten children, a stay-at-home Mother and was the heart of the home. She taught the six kids to judge not the tree, but the fruit.

Mike Kattawar, became a strong businessman that developed later in life and Dollie Kattawar, was a sensitive, nurturing Mom; the anchor of home life.

Growing up in a busy, often hectic home filled with older siblings and musical talent. It's been said that his sensitivities came from a very close relationship with his mom. Leadership, management skills and business savvy developed from close ties to his Dad. Ron chooses to say Dad was steel and Mom was velvet and he drew from the better of both.

Ron married his sweetheart from the eighth grade, Carol Cauley Kattawar. Together they parented three children, Kim, Ronnie Jr. and Jason and are now proud grandparents to Preston, C.J., Brandon, Kadence and Hailey.

You can reach Ron though his personal Facebook page or through CORNBREAD MEMORIES Facebook page.

CPSIA information can be obtained at www.ICGtesting.com
Printed in the USA
LVOW07s1656081115

461586LV00028B/1329/P